RAISING A GOOD SPORT

in an IN-YOUR-FACE World

SEVEN STEPS TO BUILDING CHARACTER
ON THE FIELD—AND OFF

George Selleck, Ph.D.

Contemporary Books

Chicago   New York   San Francisco   Lisbon   London   Madrid   Mexico City
Milan   New Delhi   San Juan   Seoul   Singapore   Sydney   Toronto

Library of Congress Cataloging-in-Publication Data

Selleck, George A. (George Abraham), 1934–.
 Raising a good sport in an in-your-face world : seven steps to building
 character on the field—and off / George Selleck.
     p.   cm.
 ISBN 0-07-139105-3
 1. Sports—Moral and ethical aspects.   2. Sportsmanship
 3. Conduct of life.   I. Title.

 GV706.3.S45   2002
 175—dc21   2002022780

Contemporary Books

A Division of The McGraw·Hill Companies

1 2 3 4 5 6 7 8 9 0   AGM/AGM   1 0 9 8 7 6 5 4 3 2

ISBN 0-07-139105-3

Cover photograph copyright © Steven Peters/Stone

McGraw-Hill books are available at special quantity discounts to use as premiums
and sales promotions, or for use in corporate training programs. For more
information, please write to the Director of Special Sales, Professional Publishing,
McGraw-Hill, Two Penn Plaza, New York, NY 10121-2298. Or contact your local
bookstore.

This book is printed on acid-free paper.

To my classmates at 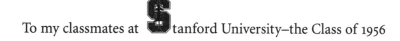tanford University–the Class of 1956

"The best portion of a good life is the little nameless,
unremembered acts of kindness and of love."
—WILLIAM WORDSWORTH

As I play out this fourth-quarter period of my life, I realize that
your gifts of kindness and warmth throughout the years have
provided the wellspring from which much of the motivation for
my work flows. This book is for all of you, with special thanks
going to:

Neil Papiano	Carlos Bea
John Stewart	R. D. Aikins
Allan Goodman	Joe Peatman
John Pearson	Norm Rich
Terry and Lynn Badger	Den Kennedy
Brad Leonard	Jerry Gustafson
Loren Mosher	Fritz Huntsinger
Tom Waterhouse	Dave Dunn
Tom and Jane Fetter	John Florida
Ron Wagner	Chuck Louden

CONTENTS

FOREWORD

In *Raising a Good Sport in an In-Your-Face World*, George Selleck invites you to join a sportsmanship revolution. He advises you to chuck the old, outdated maps you have been using during your past excursions into the world of sports. He urges you to join him in drawing a new map, one that allows you to take sport to a higher level. By taking initiatives to follow the high road you will be able to appreciate what being a good sport in today's world really means. Being a good sport will take on new meaning when you follow the road less traveled.

It is my hope that you will allow George to help you avoid the rough spots that parents typically encounter on the route to raising kids who enthusiastically embrace the highest standards of conduct in sports and beyond. George is not insisting that you follow his path. Instead, he is inviting you to step off the beaten path long enough to take in the full range of opportunities that sport is able to offer you and your family. If you choose not to follow his path, if it takes you out of your comfort zone, at the very least you will want to use his imaginative problem-solving strategies to make your sports parenting assignment less arduous.

Without a doubt you could not have chosen a better steersman to help you raise a good sport. George knows his way around the "sportscape." He understands that it is a real challenge to raise a good sport in today's "in-your-face" world. And he has come up with some very clear recommendations for helping you counter negative forces. He suggests actions you can take to help create a positive sports climate that will allow your kids to experience sport without the distractions from browbeating coaches, taunting athletes, and out-of-control parents.

George wants you to be expansive in drawing your personal map so that you will miss nothing as you prepare for the safe passage of your children through a world of sports filled with pitfalls and hazards. He does not want you to travel that road alone. He invites you to share the trip not only with your kids, but also with their teammates and coaches. It is hard to wage a battle against stubborn traditions without allying yourself with fellow travelers. He appreciates that you will need collaborators if you are to put new sports policies, practices, and traditions into place. Your partner, your kids, their teammates, and their coaches can all be recruited to join in launching a new era in sports for kids. The immediate years ahead need to be viewed as the Age of Enlightenment for sports parents, where informed and inspired moms and dads recapture sport from those warriors to whom they unwittingly relegated their parental responsibilities.

This need not be a bloody revolution. To the contrary, most members of the old guard would welcome the emergence of a new generation of sports parents who would do more than drop their kids off at the playing field, pop for a new pair of Nikes, or disrupt competitions with their crazy antics. I am convinced that coaches would fondly embrace any parents who came forward to share responsibility for raising good sports and contributing to the creation of good sports communities.

There are a few extremists—that is, staunch defenders of "in-your-face" sports, who feel the need to justify crazed coaches, athletes, and parents. It is the unwillingness of this small core of warriors to turn their backs on the dark side of sport that is spoiling sports for everyone. The defenders of "in-your-face" sports are so caught up in preserving their rights to insanity that they fail to realize the grave damage they are doing to kids, families, and, in fact, to the institution of sport they claim to cherish. Parents can take on the challenge of silencing this vocal and influential minority by including their voices in creating a new wave of sports for kids. I am convinced that the voices of the old warriors will be transformed as they come to understand how much they will benefit from having a community of parents who are invested in supporting policies that will make life more comfortable for them.

Sport can be practiced as if being orchestrated by deadly sharks establishing their dominance through intimidating their competitors. Or it can be practiced as if it were being created by playful dolphins intent upon uplifting the spirits of all those around them. The Good Sports Movement for which George has become the preeminent voice is reaching out to mobilize those sports parents who are more comfortable with dolphins than with sharks. George is inviting you to imagine an expansive future where sports empower kids, strengthen families, and enliven communities.

This does not mean that George is suggesting that sport become less competitive and that winning be discarded as a compelling goal. He wants to see sport continue to be highly competitive so that it can generate excitement, maintain the interest of all participants, and bring out the best in everyone. But he wants sport to be competitive without becoming contentious. He wants you to join his team so that you can help make sports less adult driven and more driven by the collaborative efforts of athletes, coaches, and parents. Only when the agendas of all of the main actors in the sports drama are taken into account can a sane climate of sport be established. Collaboration tends to temper extremes, and it is the excesses of a few parents, athletes, and coaches that spoil it for the many. George believes that when all of the participants in youth sports are included in establishing standards of conduct and when they are provided opportunities to commit to these standards, sportsmanship problems, as we have come to know them, will all but disappear. George believes that when mutual understanding among athletes, coaches, and parents is achieved and when they jointly commit to upholding these shared standards and values a giant step will have been taken to usher in a new era in sports.

This new era will call for a new sportsmanship, one that prizes collaboration more than obedience to rules issued from "on high." When parents, coaches, and athletes collaborate in advancing shared goals they are no longer adversaries, but instead are *partners* who have committed to making the most of their shared sports experiences.

Clearly a path less traveled is not easy to find or to follow. Today's parents would be well advised to use this book to help them discover revolutionary thinking about what sports can become for their families. Good sports are so much more than good sportsmanship. In fact, good sportsmanship becomes a by-product of collaboration when parents, athletes, and coaches establish partnerships for charting new ways of achieving their shared goals.

There are no templates that parents can buy at Sports Are Us to help them find their way to good sports experiences. Good sports cannot be discovered along some lonely road. Good sports must be created in a partnership between you, your kids, and the members of their sports communities. Every group of parents, athletes, and coaches needs to construct their own map and revisit it from time to time to make sure they are staying on course.

No one, however, has to undertake that journey through the world of sports without the benefits of guidance. I would like to offer some recommendations that may help you make the most of this book as you move along the pathway to good sports.

Know Yourself

Learn to know yourself as you evolve your own style of sports parenting. Remember that you are your own navigational instrument.

You need to learn how to master that instrument so that you can guide yourself and your kids along the pathway to becoming good sports. The first order of business is for you to understand how the instrument works—to appreciate what draws you to the style of sports parenting you have chosen. Self-awareness is of the highest order of importance in becoming an effective sports parent. Mastery of the principles outlined in this book will do you little good unless you are able to understand how you are reading them. Learn to know yourself as you evolve your own style of sports parenting.

Become an Expansive Sports Parent

If you are to become expansive in your sports parenting role so that you are able to help your kids take full advantage of what sport has to offer, you will need to learn a series of skills. The sports parenting skills that are elaborated in this book will allow you to overcome the barriers you will inevitably encounter as you move toward becoming an actualizing sports parent.

You will need to move through three phases in the process of developing into an expansive sports parent. In the first phase you will be drawn to satisfying your own needs. During that phase you will deem it of great importance to be recognized by those around you as a competent sports parent. During that phase sports parenting is all about you and affirming your worth.

During the second phase of development you will turn your attention to the welfare of your kids. At that point you will be doing everything within your power to make sure that your kids' dreams are being realized in the world of sports. Anything that stands in the way of your kids' progress will become a source of frustration. It is when parents are in this second phase of development that they become frustrated with coaches, referees, and opponents who stand in the way of their kids getting ahead. When parents are in that mind-set they are most likely to remain focused upon how they can give their kids an edge in their competition for recognition. It is then that parents' temptation is greatest to lose their cool and strike out at their kids, the coaches, the referees, or opponents whom they perceive to be standing in the way of their children's success.

In the final phase of development parents have evolved to the point where they are able to turn their attention to helping their kids' sports partners realize their dreams. Parents have progressed from being focused upon themselves, to being focused on their children, to focusing on their sports community. As they master skills during each of these phases of development they become better able to find their way so that they can serve as a competent guide to their kids. This book will help you move through this natural developmental cycle.

Examine Your State of Mind

You can ensure that you are able to provide the kind of guidance your kids deserve by investing in getting to know your own motivations. As you read through the chapters in this book it will be helpful for you to reflect upon your reactions to the ideas being offered. Rather than always judging the ideas on their logical merit, you would be well advised to ask yourself why you are responding to the ideas as you are. By engaging in self-examination as you encounter the new ideas being introduced by George you will double the return on your investment. Remember, you are your own navigational instrument on the pathway to raising good sports. You need to know yourself if you plan to stay on course.

Let me suggest that from time to time you take time out and examine your own state of mind as you encounter George's fresh ways of thinking about raising good sports. I like to think of a sports parent's state of mind as involving four major elements: viewpoint, angle of vision, motives, and images.

First of all, you have a *viewpoint* that is made up of the values you wish to promote through sports. Throughout this book you will encounter challenges that will cause you to consider shifting your value priorities regarding sports. For example, you will be invited to still cherish competition and the pursuit of winning, but you will be urged to also place value on other potential outcomes of sport, such as strengthening family ties.

Second, you choose to view sport from your own *angle of vision*. You may begin by using a telephoto lens to look at sport. You see only what is occurring on the playing field and become transfixed by the scoreboard. This narrow perspective does not allow you to take full advantage of what sport has to offer. If you can learn to look at sport through a wide-angle lens you can open up new possibilities for gaining satisfaction as you participate in the sports community. As you learn to appreciate the full range of benefits that sport can offer you, not only will you learn how to better enjoy your sports experiences, but you will also establish yourself as a better guide for your kids. This book will help you widen your angle of vision.

Third, every parent has had different life experiences that assign higher priority to some needs over others, which leads to different *motives* for sports participation. If you happen to place highest priority on satisfying your *need for achievement*, this book will invite you to also look beyond the need for achievement to the satisfaction of other needs through your sports experience. You may want to turn to sports to satisfy your *need for affiliation* by investing in using shared sports experiences to strengthen your relationships with other sports parents. Or you may want to invest in assuming a leadership role in the team community to satisfy your *need for power*. In this book you will be challenged to look for satisfaction of needs that have not previously been met through your sports parenting role.

And finally, when you were introduced to sports as a kid, you were taught to use common images, symbols, and language to organize your sports experiences. The predominant *images* used by mainstream sports come from the military where we "fight battles," "kill opponents," and "endure casualties." These images are limiting—they need to be challenged, and alternatives need to be invented. As this book causes you to reassess conventional ways of approaching sport, you may wish to invent new organizers to order your sports experiences.

George's ideas will inspire you to change your state of mind, that is, your viewpoint, angle of vision, motives, and images. As you change your state of mind you will be able to get comfortable with the revolutionary spirit created in *Raising a Good Sport*.

When you have taken steps to change your state of mind you will be motivated to equip yourself with skills that will allow you to be the kind of sports parent required in today's world. This book will help you develop the skills you need to raise good sports in an "in-your-face" world. That is the promise of this book. Let me assure you, George always keeps his promises.

—DAVID CANNING EPPERSON, PH.D.,
COFOUNDER OF PARENTS FOR GOOD SPORTS

ACKNOWLEDGMENTS

My deepest thanks to Robert Shepard of the Robert E. Shepard Agency, whose insights and guidance brought me from the grandstand onto the playing field.

And to Dave Epperson, my friend and partner in Parents for Good Sports, whose vision, support, and enthusiasm have helped me reach greater heights.

To Wendy Fayles, whose splendid talent and creativity imprints this project from beginning to end.

And to the people at Contemporary Books—truly unbeatable teammates in every respect!

INTRODUCTION

A Sportsmanship Revolution

Serious sport has nothing to do with fair play. It is bound up with hatred, jealousy, boastfulness, disregard for all rules, and sadistic pleasure in witnessing violence: in other words, it is war minus the shooting.

—GEORGE ORWELL[1]

When I first began writing this book I hoped that a lot of people would read this quote and completely disagree with it. Yet I knew in my heart that many others would read it and think, "Right on!"

Then came September 11, 2001, and people across the United States suddenly got an up-close and personal look at what war is really like. And we realized that sport—serious or otherwise—bore no resemblance whatsoever.

In the days and weeks following September 11, people reached out to each other as they never had before. Kindness became the order of the day. As we struggled to put our lives back together and return to some kind of normalcy, sport—instead of being the place where we vented our frustrations and played out our fantasies of conquest—became our refuge and our solace.

Before September 11, sports coverage tended to focus on the negative. Sadly, there were plenty of negatives to focus on. In a game played just one day before the World Trade Center incident, Banning High School in Los Angeles racked up no fewer than eight unsportsmanlike conduct penalties as they lost, 34–0, to Newhall Hart. The next day's headline in the *Los Angeles Times* trumpeted, "Banning's Unsportsmanlike Conduct Particularly Foul."

In light of everything else that would happen that day, it *was* particularly foul. Fortunately, it would be a while before we would see headlines like that again. Instead, when we turned to our sports pages we were buoyed by images like the one printed in the September 15 *Deseret News*, which showed burly football players from two arch-rival schools marching across the field hand-in-hand prior to the start of a homecoming game.

As stories of athletes raising money for victims of September's tragedy replaced stories of athletes just plain raising hell, I was not naive enough to think that this "kinder, gentler" version of sport was here to stay. The further removed we became from September 11, the more likely it was that we *would* return to normal. And in the case of sport, that was not necessarily a good thing.

Sportsmanship in Today's Society

As I worked on this book prior to September 11, there were two things that stood out in my mind when I thought about sportsmanship in today's society. The first was an incident that happened during the NBA All-Star weekend in Oakland in February 2000. Andre Miller, the outstanding point guard for the Cleveland Cavaliers, was on his way to a stellar (twenty-one points, five rebounds) game during the rookie contest. After deciding to lay the ball up off the glass instead of dunking on an easy breakaway, Miller was soundly booed by the fans. In choosing *not* to exhibit the kind of in-your-face behavior that had become synonymous with many of the current crop of professional athletes, Miller found himself in the unpopular position of spoilsport to the spectators who had assembled in the hopes of seeing the high-flying dunks and chest-thumping, trash-talking exhibition that passed for basketball at that time.

It was a classic clash between "old-world" sports values and "new-world" expectations. As a member of the old school, I naturally sympathized with Miller, whose soft-spoken personality harks back to the days of athletes who felt their main job was to score, not to entertain. On the other hand, I wouldn't have been surprised if the fans who voiced their disapproval of Miller's unspectacular play felt that *Miller* was the one who was being the poor sport—by not giving them the kind of show that they had come to expect from the NBA.

The second thing that stood out in my mind wasn't so much a single incident as a feeling that I picked up on as I traveled across the country working with parents of young athletes. What I sensed from these parents was that sport had let them down. Sport had let their kids down. Sport was supposed to be fun. It was supposed to be a way for the family to come together and enjoy each other's company and the company of their friends and neighbors. It was supposed to be a means for helping their children grow and develop and learn the important lessons of life.

Instead, sport had turned into a gut-churning, stress-inducing exercise in self-centeredness that no one ended up winning. While many reasons had been advanced for this, I felt it came down to one thing: as a society, we had moved away from the ideals and values and actions of sportsmanship. And, instead of using sport as a tool to lead us *back* to those ideals, we were dragging sport right down into the muck with us.

This worried me. It did more than that—it *scared* me. Although my own children were grown and I no longer had to worry about the impact of a win-at-all-costs coach or glory-hogging teammate on their fragile psyches, I now had grandchildren who played sports. And I knew that I would walk over broken glass—or any number of rabid fans, out-of-control parents, screaming coaches, or bloodthirsty athletes—to ensure that my grandchildren's sports experiences were positive, uplifting, and enriching.

As I passed out sportsmanship questionnaires after my workshops, the comments I received ranged from troubling to heart wrenching. In response to the question, "What are your thoughts on the state of sportsmanship in today's sports world?" one coach wrote: "Very poor. It is my single greatest area of effort." Another respondent (the wife of a youth sports coach) said, "It is pretty sad when spouses and families of coaches are so uncomfortable in the bleachers that they elect to sit away from the crowd. The foul and disparaging comments are uncomfortable for everyone and uncalled for."

I was so saddened to read comments like these. Sport provides such marvelous opportunities to help young people reach their potential, to teach them how to connect with others, and to truly attack some of the major social problems facing today's youth: alcohol and drug abuse, lack of dialogue with parents, families who don't spend time together, and now, fears of terrorism and war. But instead of using sport in this positive way, we have been allowing the negative influences of the world to infiltrate our sports experiences.

That is why I decided I had to write this book. Sport has been very good to me in my life. It was time to return the favor.

What Is Sportsmanship?

Sportsmanship. What do you think of when you hear the word? For some people, sportsmanship is nothing more than shaking your opponent's hand after a game, or not whining (too much) when you lose. I remember reading an article on human resource management that described sportsmanship as "the willingness to tolerate difficult circumstances without complaining." Others think that sportsmanship is something that just athletes are supposed to do. They don't think of it as applying to spectators, parents, or coaches.

I polled a class of fourth graders and asked them what they thought "sportsmanship" meant. Almost half of them answered, "I don't know." Others were a little more insightful:

- "I think 'sportsmanship' means that when you're doing something don't run off when you don't get your own way. That's called bad 'sportsmanship.'"
- "Sportsmanship means that even if you don't get your own way you get on with your life."
- "I think it is teamwork and working together and encouraging your teammates to do better and no put-downs so they don't leave."
- "It's like shaking a ref's hand after a game."
- "I think sportsmanship means cooperating with other members on your team like friendship."
- "It means to be a good sport and have a good time."
- "It means to be a good player. If in hockey you don't score then you skate off the ice and say 'I can never score' that is poor sportsmanship. That means you're a poor sport."
- "I think it means being a good sport and having a good attitude, being aggressive, and playing fair."
- "Don't quit a game even if your team is losing."
- "It means not to be a poor sport—that's what it means!"

Two university professors, Jennifer Beller and Sharon Kay Stoll, conducted research among college athletes to find out their definition of "sportsmanship." When asked, "What is sportsmanship?" twenty Division I football players said, "It's helping your buddies beat the other team"; "It's being a good guy for our side"; "It's speaking up for your team"; "It's supporting the team."[2] In Beller and Stoll's study of more than 150 college athletes, less than 10 percent thought that sportsmanship meant being courteous or respectful to the opposing players, though most felt that they had a duty to be fair and courteous to their own team.[3]

Taking their research a step further, Beller and Stoll reported that many high school coaches believed that when working with younger athletes (such as elementary or junior high school athletes), sportsmanship meant "shaking hands before and after the game," or "helping a teammate or opponent up when they fall."[4] However, the same coaches felt that once an athlete reached the high school or college level, such sportsmanlike actions were no longer an integral part of the game. Rather, their opinion was that sportsmanship for older athletes was something that was outdated and antiquated.[5]

I'm afraid that many people feel the same as these coaches. It's not that we consciously say, "Sportsmanship is not important anymore." It is more a case of sportsmanship not being as central to our lives as it was to individuals of another era.

But are congeniality, good manners, respect, and reaching out to others ever outdated? In light of what we have been through since September 11, I would have to say no. Even if they were, I don't believe that sport needs to be a microcosm of society, reflecting all of our ills and woes. Rather, I believe that sport can and should be a leader in helping us to achieve the kinds of families and communities that we dream about and hope for.

Fortunately, not everyone feels that sportsmanship is something that is outgrown with an athlete's Little League uniform. In their book *Coaching for Character*, Craig Clifford and Randolph M. Feezell touted a loftier definition of sportsmanship:

Sportsmanship is not just a matter of acceptable behavior but of *excellence of character*—or, in the language of the classical tradition—*sportsmanship is a virtue*. . . . Sportsmanship, then, is not just about following rules, behaving a certain way because that's the way you're supposed to behave; it's about what sort of human beings we choose to become.[6]

Russell W. Gough, a professor of philosophy and ethics at Pepperdine University, spoke of sportsmanship as "a matter of being good (character) and doing right (action) in sports."[7]

Baron Pierre de Coubertin, the originator of the modern Olympic Games, felt that sport was something that could be used to help the young people of the world "become better acquainted with the nations and peoples of other countries without regard to sex, race, color, or religious beliefs."[8] De Coubertin's feeling was that, through disciplining the body, mind, and spirit, athletes could come to a better understanding of themselves and the right way to live. In other words, they could become better sportsmen and sportswomen. This feeling is summarized in the five ideals that were established as a part of the first modern Olympic Games held in 1896:

- To help develop better citizens through the building of character that accompanies participation in amateur sports.
- To demonstrate the principles of fair play and good sportsmanship.
- To stimulate interest in fine arts through exhibitions, concerts, and demonstrations during the games, and in so doing contribute to a well-rounded life.
- To teach that sports are played for fun and enjoyment.
- To create international friendship and goodwill that would lead to a happier and more peaceful world.[9]

To de Coubertin, Gough, Clifford, and Feezell, sportsmanship isn't something that only has relevance on the playing field; rather, it is an integral part of a person's character, and as such, cannot afford to be overlooked or downplayed by parents whose children play sports.

The irony is that for all its differences in interpretation, sportsmanship is still something that is easier to talk about than to practice. For example, I think if you were to ask any parent if sportsmanship is an important quality for athletes to have, no one would disagree. Most parents *say* that they believe sportsmanship is important. However, what people say and what people do is not always the same—as witnessed by the many noteworthy examples of unsportsmanlike behavior on the part of parents themselves.

In addition, one person's idea of sportsmanship isn't necessarily another's. One parent may believe that sportsmanship means following every rule to the letter. Another parent may feel that certain rules should be followed, but others can be stretched. Athletes and coaches may have their own differing opinions.

I feel it is crucial that this book doesn't just provide a definition of sportsmanship, but creates a definition that goes beyond shaking hands and playing fair. Thus, my primary objectives in this book are to:

- Redefine sportsmanship as more than just good manners, to include everything that is good and worthy about sports. In other words, I want to draw a new sportsmanship "map," because the old one can no longer get us where we need to go.
- Take sportsmanship beyond the abstract and turn it into something that is concrete and doable by describing specific actions that parents can take in order to raise the bar of sportsmanship in their children and themselves.

- Connect sportsmanship to real life. In a survey released by America's Promise and the Gallup Organization, Americans said that preparing young people for the future should be the nation's priority. That is what sportsmanship can do. It can lay the groundwork for lives that are productive and meaningful. The same actions that young people learn to use to become better sports are the actions that can help them learn how to effectively deal with such problems as disagreements with family members, disenfranchised fellow students, misunderstandings between people of different cultures, and so forth.
- Help parents accept responsibility for the problem. Before we can solve a problem, we have to take responsibility for it. That doesn't necessarily mean saying, "It's all my fault." It means saying, "It doesn't really matter whose fault it is, I'm going to start doing my part to fix it."
- Get parents thinking about what they expect from sports and how they can get it. Too many parents go into the whole youth sports thing without really thinking about it. They sign their kids up, buy the uniforms, show up for the games, and never stop to think beforehand about what they want their children to learn from the experience and how they will help them learn it.
- Give parents a tool they can use to define the values they hold important and want to impart to their children.
- Show parents how they can partner with their children in using sport as a training ground to examine family values, reflect on what is important to them as a family, and work together to solve problems that occur in sports and life.
- Maximize the potential of sport and minimize the dangers. I built a whole nonprofit agency (Sports for Life, Inc.) centered on the belief that every life skill necessary for a productive

and successful life can be learned from sports. But sport can do even more than teach our children how to be a team player or develop a winning attitude. Sport can strengthen families and communities. It can build bridges between individuals from diverse backgrounds. It can inspire. It can uplift. It can be a connector and a healer. It all starts with sportsmanship.

Sportsmanship Begins at Home

Why is this book addressed to parents rather than coaches or athletes? As Pat Woodall, a twenty-five-year veteran coach and officiator, says, "Sportsmanship begins in the home." Athletes will go through a succession of coaches in their lives, all with varying viewpoints and philosophies on sportsmanship. Parents, however, are the ones who are there through all the ups and downs and wins and losses, providing their athletic children with a consistent message and model of what it means to be a good sport. An athlete who learns sportsmanship in the home will not need to relearn it on the playing field.

I understand that today's parents are busy. You are stressed. You are overcommitted and overextended. I recognize that. These are pressures I feel in my own life. But I can guarantee that if you take the time to read this book and apply its principles to your own life and the lives of your children, it will make life a whole lot easier—and better—in the long run.

In this way, sportsmanship is like sewing a garment. Sometimes you don't want to take the time to do the measuring, the pinning, the basting. So you skip some of those preparatory steps that lay the foundation for the finished product. And then you either end up with a garment that is less than desirable, or you spend more time trying to fix the mistakes than it would have taken to do things right to start with.

Doing sportsmanship "right" from the beginning is important because sportsmanship is not just a desirable attribute for the athletic field. It's not something that only affects children during that brief time they take to the field or the court. Sportsmanship provides children with basic principles and values that can guide them in their sports activities and beyond, ensuring that sport is not merely a destination—a skill to be learned, a championship to be won—but a journey that contributes greatly to the richness and meaning of their lives.

Enjoy the Journey

Why is the concept of sport as a journey such an important one? As someone who has spent many, many years in the counseling field, I can tell you that the majority of patients' problems stem from the habit they have of living either in the past or in the future. What they need to do is focus on the present. A person who is living in the present—enjoying each moment, instead of dwelling on what was or wishing for what might be—is much more likely to be a happy, healthy person.

In the same way, many of the problems of sports—and sportsmanship—could be solved if individuals would live in the present of their sports experience. If parents stopped dwelling on their unfulfilled childhood sports dreams and just relished being able to watch their children play, we would have no need for "Silent Sundays" or parental sportsmanship contracts. If kids stopped counting on the possibility of getting a scholarship or a professional contract and enjoyed the satisfaction that comes with being able to learn and develop their skills, we would see fewer stress injuries and more well-rounded athletes. If coaches stopped focusing so much on the win and started focusing more on the fun, we wouldn't see children dropping out of sports in record numbers.

None of this needs to take away from the intensity of sports. Rather, it would change it from an intensity of pressure to an intensity of joy.

And if we could come to view sport as a journey—sport, with all its emphasis on results and finishes and statistics—then how much better would we be at seeing life in the same light! Today's broken heart, tomorrow's lost job—they would still be painful, but not insurmountable.

Victor Hugo said, "An invasion of armies can be resisted, but not an idea whose time has come." I believe that the need to revolutionize sports—and sportsmanship—is an idea whose time has come.

Whether we are living in the worst of times or the best of times depends on your perspective; however, it is clear we are living in radically changing times. Around the globe, entire societies are in the midst of dramatic change. And our young people are feeling the effects of this change. They are under more stress and more pressure than ever before. Violence, school shootings, alcohol and drugs, teenage pregnancy, and other crises of values puncture their world.

The world of sports is no different. It continues to be transformed under the pervasive influence of the professional sports model where winning takes precedence over participation, fair play, and personal and social development. Despite all this, sport remains one of our greatest opportunities to meet young people "where they are at," introduce them to positive values, and support their growth and maturation into caring, responsible human beings.

It will take nothing less than a revolution—one that would humanize sport and free it from the professional model and its values. It is not a matter of attempting to turn the clock back to the days of sandlot baseball games and "Leave It to Beaver" neighborhoods. Rather, it is a matter of moving forward, of moving beyond the "winning is the most important thing" philosophy of today's sports to instead view and experience sport as part of the journey to becoming and being good people, not just good sports.

Ideally, what we are trying to do is not just "fix" sport—we are trying to fix society *through* sport. For too long it has been said that sport reflects society. Sport can do more than that. We can make it do more than that. Instead of a reflection, we can make sport a beacon, pointing the way to a brighter future and a better world for our children and for generations of children to come.

Actions of a Good Sport

Because of the competitive process practiced in America, athletes learn "not to think" about the weighty issues of ethics. Instead, they blindly and passively follow the accepted behavioral norms. If everyone else practices behavior A and wins, we will practice behavior A.
—ANGELA LUMPKIN, SHARON KAY STOLL, AND
JENNIFER M. BELLER, *SPORTS ETHICS*[1]

When I was a kid, sport was a tool for keeping us off the street and giving us something fun to do. In today's world, sport needs to be more than that. Today, kids are bombarded with things that were virtually nonexistent when I was growing up. Television shows are becoming increasingly realistic in their portrayals of violence and immorality. Video games have "evolved" from Pacman to Mortal Kombat III. The Internet offers easy access to every kind of sickness and sadism imaginable—and some that are even beyond imagining.

As a parent, you need all the help you can get in equipping your children to deal with a world that is often difficult and threatening. So when you stand behind your son or daughter and gently place your hands over your child's as you show him or her how to hold a bat or shoot a free throw, remember that you need to teach your children more than just the actions of sport. You need to teach them the actions of sportsmanship. Through learning and doing these critical actions, your children will be better prepared to make good choices and decisions throughout their lives as they meet the challenges of dealing with an "in-your-face" world.

From Words to Action

Unfortunately, most competitive people are so involved in personal and professional activities, whether practicing a sport, preparing for a game, studying for classes, visiting with friends, or just making it through the day, that thinking about fundamental moral issues seems unimportant.

—ANGELA LUMPKIN, SHARON KAY STOLL,
AND JENNIFER M. BELLER, *SPORTS ETHICS*[2]

I hold four degrees—two from Stanford, one from Princeton, and one from the University of Southern California. Twelve years of college and I never *really* learned a thing. Why? Because I was a fast-food learner. I would quickly pick up the information I needed in order to pass a test, and just as quickly forget it once the test was over. My goal was to make good grades because I thought having good grades meant you were a smart person. In my case, all it meant was that I had good short-term memory.

What I *did* learn from school is that when it comes to real learning—learning that stays with you for a lifetime—words are not enough. You have to have action. You have to *do.* You have to put things to work. You have to see how they apply to you. Just as you cannot learn to play basketball by reading about it, you cannot learn to be a good sport by talking about it. It requires putting it into action.

Sport is an active process. So, too, is sportsmanship. In order to *be* a good sport and raise children who are good sports, you need to actively work to create change within your children and yourself.

Therein lies the challenge: How do you take a bunch of idealistic words and thoughts and actually motivate someone to do them? Is it even possible to implement the kind of sportsmanship that I advocate in this book? I believe it is, or I wouldn't waste the effort of writing. Not only do I believe it *is* possible to create a new sportsmanship, I believe that doing so is absolutely critical to the future of sport. As it stands now, kids are dropping out of organized sports programs in record numbers. Television viewership for many professional sports competitions continues to decline. As sport—both amateur and professional—has become increasingly focused on showmanship and winning, it has lost the heart of the people. I believe that an increased emphasis on sportsmanship would go a long way toward putting the heart back.

I have determined that there are seven crucial actions that good sports need to implement in order to create the kind of sportsmanship that is necessary to revolutionize sport and improve its influence on society. These steps are:

1. Know how to lose
2. Understand the difference between winning and success
3. Respect others
4. Cooperate with others
5. Show integrity
6. Exhibit self-confidence
7. Give back

These actions are all part of the process of changing sport from the inside out. They are not designed to be temporary, stopgap measures. They have nothing to do with adding more rules to the rule book. On the other hand, they have *everything* to do with making the kind of inner changes that make a lasting difference in an individual's life.

Model–Teach–Encourage

To help you put what you learn in this book into action, I have provided special "Model-Teach-Encourage" sections at the ends of Chapters Two through Eight. These sections provide you with different tips and special activities designed to help you use the information provided in the chapters to build positive sports behavior in your children. The sections are based on the premise that the best way to influence another person's behavior is to model, teach, and encourage change.

Model
Imitation is the most basic form of learning. From the time they are tiny infants, our children are continually watching us and mimicking what we do. A friend of mine told of walking into the bathroom one night to check on her five-year-old son, who was taking a bath. As she went to wash his face, she noticed that his chin was bleeding. "Spencer, what did you do to yourself?" she asked, thinking that perhaps he had fallen in the tub and bumped his chin. Shamefaced, he pulled a razor from beneath the bubbles. "I wanted to shave like Daddy," he replied.

Not only do children learn *first* by example, they also learn *best* by example. So when it comes to teaching sportsmanship, you must lead the way by modeling the kind of positive actions you want them to take. If you don't, then all of your other teaching will be in vain. That's because children are quick to sniff out hypocrisy of any kind. For instance, I have two grandsons, ages five and three, with whom I spend a lot of time. Whenever we get into the car to go somewhere—even if it's just around the corner to the convenience store—they watch me like two beady-eyed little hawks to make sure I put my seat belt on. You see, since I grew up in an era when the importance of wearing seat belts wasn't emphasized as much as it is now, there are times when I forget to buckle up. And to be truthful, there are times when I just don't want to bother. But Christian and Cayleb have had it drilled into them by the adults in their lives that "the car doesn't go unless your seat belts are fastened." If I try to get away with driving unbuckled, the next thing I hear is an accusatory chorus from the backseat: "Papa! You forgot to put your seat belt on!" And so I dutifully pull the strap across my chest and slide the buckle into its slot—not because I'm worried about my personal safety, but because I know if I don't, the next time I try to go anywhere with my grandsons they're going to insist that they don't have to wear their seat belts, either.

It was Emerson who originated the saying, "Your actions speak so loudly I can't hear what you are saying." Our actions do speak louder than our words. That is why modeling is the first important principle of raising good sports.

Teach

On the other hand, just because you are modeling a behavior you can't assume that your children are automatically learning it. You also need to actively look for opportunities to illustrate and reinforce the behavior you want them to exhibit. This is teaching.

Take the seat belt situation, for example. Eventually, Christian and Cayleb will reach the age where they will be able to decide for themselves whether they will wear seat belts or not. At that point, "just because Grandpa does it" is not going to be a strong enough reason for them to continue doing so. In fact, it might even be a reason for them *not* to do it. After all, how many sixteen-year-old boys want to be just like their grandfathers? That's why, in addition to giving them the "no seat belt—no go" rule, I make a point to talk to them about why it's important for us to wear seat belts. If I have to stop the car suddenly (which never fails to elicit shrieks of, "That was fun, Papa! Do it again!"), I might casually ask them what they thought might have happened if they hadn't been wearing their seat belts at that moment. If we pass a car wreck on the freeway, I always say, "Gee, I hope those people were wearing their seat belts."

In other words, I try to get my grandsons to really think about the reasons for wearing a seat belt and the consequences of not wearing one. I try to get them to do the kind of thinking that I failed to do when I was in college. Because of their young ages I do want them to accept many things on my say-so, but I also want them to learn how to make good choices when I'm not around. To do that, they need to be able to think things through for themselves.

As you teach the seven actions of a good sport, remember that the goal is for your children to become willing and enthusiastic partners with you in the sportsmanship revolution. This means that, as in any true partnership, preaching and lecturing need to be replaced with listening and understanding.

A sure sign of an inexperienced teacher (or an inexperienced parent) is one who does nothing but talk, talk, talk. Research shows that among university students, the ability to retain information falls off substantially after ten to twenty minutes. With younger children, the time span is even shorter (with my grandsons, I think it's about five seconds). Thus, a wise teacher is one who presents information and then listens, prods, and challenges the student to do something with that information.

To sum things up, great teachers don't teach; they help kids teach themselves. It requires more effort on the teacher's part, but

the payoff is worth it. That is why teaching is the second important principle of raising good sports.

Encourage

When you remember to use positive reinforcement, you will find
that children are more likely to enjoy the challenge of rising to a
new level of sportsmanship in their lives. And if they enjoy it,
they're more likely to do it.

Phil Jackson, coach of the Los Angeles Lakers, often talks about
how the effectiveness of his players increased when he started
making an effort to say more positive things to them. It was hard,
because as a coach he was used to criticizing most of the things
his players did. But he began trying to balance every negative criticism with several supportive, encouraging comments. At first,
Jackson didn't really believe that doing this would have much of
an effect on grown-up, professional ballplayers, but he was surprised. It made a *big* difference.

If this method has such a profound effect on adults, just think
of how it will work with children. The key is to remember what
the word *encourage* means. Literally, it means to "give courage."
And courage is precisely what your children will need if they are
going to go against the grain of the current accepted levels of
sportsmanship to set a higher standard.

So remember, for every time you find yourself saying, "Susie, I
was very disappointed at the way you argued with the referee
today," you need to balance that with encouragement, as in the
following:

- "I liked the way you helped your opponent up after she fell."
- "I thought you did a great job of passing the ball to your
  teammates so they could have more opportunities to shoot."
- "I appreciated the way you sincerely congratulated the other
  players after you lost."

A helpful way of remembering to encourage your children is to remind yourself to always offer them "instructional sandwiches." The recipe for an instructional sandwich is this:

1. Comment on what the child has done right. ("When the coach benched you, I appreciated the way you sat down without making a big scene. That showed a lot of respect for your coach and your teammates.")
2. Let the child know what he or she can do to improve. ("You could show even more respect by cheering for your replacement when he/she is playing.")
3. Finish with another positive comment that will motivate the child. ("I've seen a big improvement in the team's sportsmanship this year, and I think a lot of it is because of your example. Keep up the good work!")

There is one last point I want to make on the subject of encouragement. I have found that I am much better at encouraging my grandchildren than I was at encouraging my children's sports performance. Why? I think it's because as a grandparent I am more relaxed. When my children were in sports, I was seldom able to relax and enjoy the experience. I was anxious about how they would perform; I was apprehensive about the possibility that they might get hurt; I was worried that every misstep or misdeed on their part would reflect poorly on my parenting skills or on the athletic genes that I had passed down to them. In other words, I was a pretty typical sports parent. Whether I was trying to teach my kids how to shoot a basket or complete a math problem, my anxiety over whether they would "get it" was something that my kids easily picked up on. At that point, out went the fun and in came the pressure.

So as you encourage your children, examine your motives. If your reason for trying to improve your children's sportsmanship is so that others will think well of them or of you, then you will probably experience the same kind of anxiety that I did—and your encouragement will come across as pressure. But if you are trying to raise the level of sportsmanship in your children because you know that doing so will help them have happier, more fulfilling sports experiences, then there will be less pressure on them to prove themselves to anyone but themselves.

A Final Reason for Sportsmanship

It's relatively easy to work on personalities: all we have to do is learn some new skill, rearrange language patterns, adopt human relations technologies, employ visualization affirmations, or strengthen our self-esteem. But it's comparatively hard to change habits, develop virtues, learn basic disciplines, keep promises, be faithful to vows, exercise courage, or be genuinely considerate of the feelings and convictions of others. Nonetheless, it's the true test and manifestation of our maturity.
—STEPHEN COVEY, *PRINCIPLE-CENTERED LEADERSHIP*[3]

No child is born knowing all the rules of etiquette and good behavior. Learning about these is a process. During this process our children will test all the rules—family rules, society's rules, and rules of nature. It is our job as parents to guide our kids during this process to teach them right from wrong, and help them move toward adulthood, giving each developmental stage its due.
—ELIZABETH PANTLEY, *KID COOPERATION*[4]

The ultimate (and bittersweet) goal of parenting is to prepare your children to live without you. To do that, you need to help them develop maturity. *Sportsmanship* and *maturity* are virtually interchangeable terms. As one grows, so does the other.

As you seek to apply the model-teach-encourage principles in raising your children to be good sports, you also need to keep in mind that as your children grow they go through different developmental stages. Just because your five-year-old pouts and cries when he strikes out doesn't mean you've failed in your quest to teach sportsmanship. And it certainly doesn't mean he's going to act the same way when he's fifteen. It is perfectly normal for five-year-olds to pout and cry. That's just what they *do*.

At the lowest level of maturity, children naturally tend to be pretty self-centered. Consequently, when you watch a game of soccer or basketball between a bunch of very young players, one of the most common refrains you hear is "Give *me* the ball!" Rarely will you hear a player saying, "Hey, Elise is wide open; pass it to her!"

When children this age do exhibit sportsmanship, it's generally because they are told to do so by some authority figure, such as a parent or a coach. They obey because they know if they don't, there will most likely be some kind of punishment. ("If I throw my racket again my mom won't let me play.") But if they can get away with breaking a rule without getting caught, they usually have little hesitation in doing so.

As athletes grow and enter the second level of maturity, they are more likely to exhibit sportsmanlike behavior because they want to do those things that will make them look good in the eyes of other people. They understand that, as a society, we generally favor good guys over bad guys. In addition, athletes begin to feel that there is an unwritten contract among opponents to treat each other as you would want to be treated. ("People would probably see me if I spit in my opponent's swimming lane, so I'd better not do it. Plus, I don't want *her* spitting in *my* lane, either.")

Finally, at the third, or highest, level of maturity you have athletes who have a genuine interest in the well-being of others. They understand that in the long run, for any single person to benefit, the welfare of the entire group must come first—even if it means personal sacrifice on their own part. At this level, athletes exhibit sportsmanship of the highest caliber. ("My teammates are going to hate me, but I can't lie about touching that ball before it went out of bounds. It wouldn't be fair to the other team, or to the game.")

In summary, athletes at the first level of thinking do the right thing because they're afraid not to; athletes at the second level do the right thing because they want other people to think highly of them; and athletes at the third level do the right thing because it is simply the right thing to do. They know that, in the end, doing the right thing serves the greater good.

In my monthly coaching workshops for new high school coaches, I try to emphasize the need to see kids from a developmental perspective—meaning they grow and develop in stages, and the coach's job is to move them further along the continuum. Sometimes coaches who don't have a lot of experience with kids tend to see them in absolutes: "She's a good kid. He's a bad kid. Hence, I can work with her, but I can't work with him." The truth is, none of us are absolutes. None of us can be considered "finished" as human beings until the day we die. Until then, we are all in various stages of development and we will continue to move from one stage to another.

To this end, I have tried to include tips and activities in the "Model-Teach-Encourage" sections that can be applied to a range of ages and maturity levels. You will need to use your discretion in adapting these to fit the needs and abilities of your children.

Ultimately, maturity in a human being involves the ability to look beyond one's own selfish desires to try to understand and do what's right for everyone. In the sportsmanship revolution, the new sportsmanship requires following the same path. Until now, sportsmanship has primarily been relegated to the first and second levels of maturity. I propose that we take sportsmanship to the next level, where it will hopefully become more than something that athletes feel they *ought* to do. It will become something they *want* to do.

Sportsmanship Makes Every Sports Experience Meaningful

I'll never forget a few years ago watching two college football teams play their last game of the season. Since bowl berths had already been assigned and nothing hinged on the outcome of the game, the television sports announcers kept referring to it as "meaningless."

That really disturbed me. Sport is only meaningful if something is at stake? What about playing to improve your skills? What about playing to provide entertainment for the fans? What about playing just for the sheer joy of being able to run around outside on a gorgeous fall day? Aren't these things meaningful?

One of the valuable lessons that children learn from sport is how to set and achieve goals. At the same time, one of the drawbacks of sport is that it is so goal oriented. And, more often than not, the main goal of sports is to win. Players, teams, coaches, and fans become so caught up in the destination of sports—the championship, the title, the winning season—that they forget to enjoy the journey.

This quality isn't unique to sports. It's something people tend to do throughout their lives. We tell ourselves, "When I graduate (or get a new car or a better job or a big promotion), *then* I will be happy." What we forget is that happiness is supposed to be something we feel along the way. It's not supposed to be our reward for finally getting there.

As a former minister, I am reminded of what is said in the 118th Psalm: "This is the day the Lord hath made; we will rejoice and be glad in it." You don't have to be religious or believe in God to get the point that's being made here. The same theme has been expressed over and again in countless ways. "Stop and smell the roses." "Today is the first day of the rest of your life."

Given this perspective, there are no meaningless sports competitions. Each competition, regardless of what is at stake, is an opportunity for athletes to develop their skills, grow from the experience, connect with others, and celebrate shared moments. As you model, teach, and encourage the seven actions of a good sport, you will find that you and your children will gain greater meaning from participating in sport, and it will become a more joyful journey for all of you.

Rejoice and be glad in it.

A Good Sport Knows How to Lose

Failing at something is the best way to learn what it takes to succeed at it.

—SUMMER SANDERS, *CHAMPIONS ARE RAISED, NOT BORN*[1]

It was Andy Rooney who said, "The only bad thing about being a good sport is that you have to lose to prove it." While that is not exactly true (it can be just as challenging for winners to be good sports—just ask all those Lakers fans who rioted in the streets of Los Angeles after their team won the 2000 NBA Championship), it *is* true that one of the first things we associate with sportsmanship is losing.

It's sad that losing holds such a negative connotation in our society, because it is through losing, much more than winning, that we can become stronger, smarter, better people. A good sport recognizes that fact, and seeks to capitalize on it.

Knowing How to Lose: A Three-Pronged Approach

Is it possible to be a successful loser? Certainly. The late Charles Schulz, creator of "Peanuts," was eminently successful at drawing his cartoon of a lovable loser primarily because he had so much firsthand experience at losing. Schulz did poorly in school, flunking every subject in the eighth grade. He made the school's golf team and promptly lost the most important match of the season. His cartoons were rejected by the editor of his high school yearbook, and later by Walt Disney Studios.[2] At that point, Schulz could have raged at the world, sent off scathing letters to Disney executives, and beat up the hapless yearbook editor. Instead, he did none of those things. He quietly filed away each experience under that heading we call "life," and used them to create a character that everybody loved because everybody could identify with—Charlie Brown.

Being a good loser is probably the hardest thing in life to do. At the same time, I think it's interesting that many of the greatest individuals in history have also been notable losers. Albert Einstein couldn't pass his college entrance exams. Michael Jordan was cut from the varsity squad in his sophomore year of high school. Abraham Lincoln lost jobs, lost his business, and lost election after election—but he never quit trying, and he never quit learning. Obviously, there is value in losing. The challenge is to help our children see that value.

Generally, when we call someone a "good loser," we mean that he or she is upbeat (or at least composed) in the face of a loss. He or she doesn't throw the game pieces on the floor, doesn't badmouth the person who got the promotion instead of him or her, and doesn't refuse to shake hands with an opponent. So the first, and most critical, part of knowing how to lose involves learning how to exercise self-control under what can often be daunting circumstances.

However, try telling that to a ten-year-old goalie whose teammates are all mad at him because he has just let the puck ricochet off his stick and into the net, allowing the winning score. At that point, he doesn't *want* to be a good loser. He doesn't *want* to exercise self-control. He just wants to hit something! Or cry, or complain endlessly about how unfair life is.

This is where understanding the value of losing comes in. Thus, the second part of knowing how to lose involves turning losing into a positive experience by looking for the lessons that can be learned from the loss. This is what I call being a "smart loser."

Finally, knowing how to lose involves learning how to "let it go" so that you are prepared to move on, unencumbered, to the next experience. This is the most difficult part of all. Not only is it difficult to do, but the child who actually manages to accomplish it is sometimes chastised by teammates (or coaches, or even parents) as "not caring" about his or her mistakes or the team's loss.

Knowing how to lose is a key attribute to being able to successfully negotiate your way not just through sports, but also through life. As a parent, part of your job is to equip your children to meet life's failures with equanimity. This chapter will help you learn how to do so.

Exercising Self-Control

I couldn't stop thinking how awful this was for Janet. To lose her gold-medal event to me, an upstart, a newcomer! I couldn't imagine it. She was unseated. Her reign as champion was over. Finito.

Yet there she stood, calmly answering Rowdy's questions, holding it together like I don't think I could have then, in her position. She could have ducked out of the interview, could have said she didn't want to talk; she could have climbed out of the pool and run off and cried or slammed her fist against a wall or any of a thousand things I've seen swimmers do after losing a big race. When Rowdy asked her what happened out there, she could have claimed some excuse, found someone or something to blame. But instead she said, "Summer swam a great race."

I never forgot the way she handled her defeat.

            —SUMMER SANDERS (DISCUSSING HER DEFEAT OF OLYMPIC
MEDALIST JANET EVANS), *CHAMPIONS ARE RAISED, NOT BORN*[3]

*We don't know how to handle conflict with dignity, we just don't. It's
a critical skill, but you tell me who's teaching it to our children.*

        —MARY PENNELL, VICE PRESIDENT, SAN DIEGO MEDIATION CENTER[4]

What is self-control? It is a skill we learn that enables us to suppress undesirable, inappropriate behaviors and act in a socially acceptable way. Self-control isn't something a person is born with. It's a quality we develop over time. Unfortunately, it seems like these days it's taking more time for people to develop self-control than it used to. And apparently some of us aren't developing it at all.

In a *USA Today* article discussing what appears to be a growing national trend toward a lack of self-control in sports, William Doherty, a professor of family social science at the University of Minnesota, notes, "Some individuals who don't have very much emotional impulse control go over the edge." And as the number of kids in sports increases, "you've got thousands of parents along for the ride."

In the same article, James Garbarino, human development professor at Cornell University, says, "There is a general breakdown of social conventions, of manners, of social controls. This gives a validation, a permission, to be aggressive." Kids used to be "guided by a social convention that said 'keep the lid on.' Today they are guided more in the direction of taking it off."[5]

In other words, people look at shows such as "Jerry Springer" and think, "Hey, I have the right to say what I want to say!" And if words don't work, then they feel like they have the right to back it up with violence. When enough people exhibit this kind of lack of self-control, the result is youth sports leagues that feel the need to sponsor good sportsmanship programs and take other anti-violence measures. This is a sad commentary on the state of sports in America, according to Michael S. Josephson, founder and president of the Josephson Institute of Ethics. "I think that sports is becoming more and more an arena where people are allowing unrestrained anger and passion to play out," Josephson said. "We don't know how to control violence. We are more and more moving from sport to spectacle."[6]

To help your children recognize the importance of self-control, you need to make sure they understand the consequences of losing it. Losing composure during a game, for example, doesn't just brand a person as a poor sport. It can have serious consequences for the athlete and his or her team. When Tie Domi purposely whacked an opponent in the face with his elbow during the final seconds of an NHL game, the opponent was hauled out of the rink on a stretcher. Domi was then suspended for the playoffs. With one unthinking act, Domi managed to hurt his opponent, himself, his team, and his sport's reputation.

Lack of self-control can also tarnish you for a lifetime. In 1977, Kermit Washington of the Los Angeles Lakers punched Houston's Rudy Tomjanovich during a game at the Forum. Tomjanovich's skull was fractured and his jaw and nose broken. Washington had gotten into a scuffle with another player when Tomjanovich rushed to the other player's defense. Feeling threatened, Washington threw the almost-fatal punch. He has not thrown another punch since. However, despite the fact that his life has been devoted to a variety of good works, including ten relief missions to war-torn areas in Africa, what people remember is the punch, and that distresses Washington. "I just don't want to die like this," he said. "I just don't want everyone remembering me for something negative."[7]

John McEnroe, never noted for his self-control on the court, has admitted that his temper might have kept him from winning several major titles. One of his more costly mistakes occurred at the 1990 Australian Open when he lost by default because of his abusive language. "It was embarrassing because I had two little kids with me when I was leaving the airport," McEnroe said. "Everybody was taking my picture. That was the only time in my career I was defaulted. It should have happened a couple of other times, but no one had the guts to deal with it. Part of what made me succeed was that drive, that inner intensity, but there's a way of smoothing the rough edges. Clearly, I think it hurt me at times."[8]

More recently, Atlanta's John Rocker was America's poster boy for lack of self-control. The Braves' infamous relief pitcher exchanged taunts with New York fans during the 1999 World Series, zapped the city and its inhabitants in a subsequent interview with *Sports Illustrated*, and later tried to intimidate the writer who did the interview. Teammates and Braves administration bemoaned Rocker's apparent lack of ability to adhere to the old adage, "If you can't say anything nice, don't say anything at all." To the day he dies, Rocker will probably be known as "that bigmouth baseball player."

What is it that enables some people to put up with frustration, disappointment, or anger without lashing out, while others hit back, either verbally or physically, at the first sign of opposition? I have found that children who exhibit self-control generally have one or more of the following:

• **High self-esteem.** Children who lose control and lash out during a game often do so because something has happened to make them feel bad about themselves. Feeling bad about yourself is different from feeling frustrated that you missed a basket. A child who feels frustrated that she missed a basket will say, "Man, that was a stupid mistake." On the other hand, a child with low self-esteem will say, "Man, *I'm* so stupid!"

Children with high self-esteem recognize that you can make mistakes and it doesn't mean you're a bad person or a stupid person. This allows them to shrug off the mistake faster, and not be permanently affected by it. It also allows them to be less intimidated by the idea of losing, or "looking bad" in front of others.

• **Commitment to a value.** This doesn't have to be a religious value, although often it is. Whatever the value is, it is important enough that the child wants to represent that value to others. He or she wants to be a good example. Even though at sixty-seven I am far from my childhood years, it is my commitment to the value of sportsmanship that helps me keep my mouth shut during my afternoon basketball pickup games. And let me tell you, it's not easy! A lot of the guys I play with think the purpose of the game is to get a shot rather than outscore the opponent. Consequently, they fire away any time they have the ball in their hands, rather than pass the ball to someone else in order to set up a high percentage shot. It requires a lot of self-restraint on my part not to shoot off a snide remark, or start hogging the ball myself.

• **An understanding of their personal "hot buttons."** Ninety percent of self-control is just being able to recognize the things that set you off in the first place. For example, most mothers know that kids who get whiny and combative right before dinner are usually doing so because they're hungry. It's a fact that children simply need to be fed more often than adults. So smart moms don't say, "Don't touch that cookie! Don't you know it's almost dinnertime?" Instead, they say, "Here, honey, have a banana. That will help you feel better."

As a parent, you can help your children recognize those particular things that are more likely to cause them to lose their cool during sports. For instance, I know one young athlete who hated for anyone to talk to her after she made a mistake. Even saying something encouraging like, "Good effort! Don't worry, you'll get it next time!" was enough to send her into a rage. Basically, she needed time to process her feelings and work through them on her own before dealing with anyone else. Once she recognized this, she was able to control her feelings a little bit better. And once her parents recognized this, they were able to help her out by giving her space.

• **The ability to handle stress.** Unfortunately, it's not enough just to recognize your hot buttons; you have to be able to defuse them, too. Most kids (especially younger ones) need adult help with this. At school, teachers talk to kids about acceptable ways of expressing anger and frustration, but they might need your help in transferring these techniques from the classroom to the athletic field. You can also help by emphasizing effort over results. If your kids get the sense from you that *trying* is more important than *winning*, then a good deal of the pressure that goes with playing sports will be relieved.

• **A sense of personal responsibility.** Lack of self-control has been blamed on everything from genetic makeup to that ever-popular excuse "the devil made me do it." For example, in a basketball game between Brigham Young University and the University of Arizona, Arizona player Eugene Edgerson decided to retaliate against BYU's Bret Jepsen for a couple of physical exchanges under the basket. Edgerson waited at midcourt and purposely struck Jepsen with an elbow to the face as Jepsen was running to the other end of the floor. Jepsen was knocked unconscious, suffering a severe concussion that eventually ended his college basketball career and still affects him to this day. At one point, Edgerson tried to approach his fallen rival. "I wanted to apologize," he said. "I was worried. I just didn't realize what I had done. I really didn't mean to do it. I was going to hit him—there's no doubt about that. But I didn't want to hit him that hard. When I went to the bench, I thought, man, I did some serious damage. It was like some evil got into me."[9]

A similar, but even more chilling, situation happened between two fathers after a youth hockey practice. One father, angered at what he thought was rough play on the part of some of the players, "had words" with another father who was on the ice supervising. The belligerent dad, Thomas Junta, was escorted out of the rink, but returned shortly afterward. At that point, Junta physically assaulted the other father, slamming his head into the cement floor. Thus, at age forty, Michael Costin went from being a sports dad to a sports statistic—the first known parent to be killed by another in a fit of sports rage.

After Costin's death, commentators were quick to point to societal factors as possible contributors to Junta's lack of control. While it is true that society may have played a part, I agree with what columnist Diana Griego Erwin wrote in the *Sacramento Bee*:

A national wringing of hands over a so-called culture of rage will not explain this. The problem isn't a social disease; it's not what the individual has, it's what he hasn't.

An inner voice is what's missing here, and it seems to be woefully absent in too many places. Still, most of us still have one.

It's that calming influence that you listen to when you think about ramming that car that cut you off on the freeway. It whispers, "Yeah, right. Your insurance company would love that."

It's the voice of reason, the one that stops us from doing some of those crazy things that pop into our heads.[10]

The point is, *most* parents are not beating each other to death over a children's game, just as *most* basketball players aren't running around intentionally inflicting enough damage to end another person's career. Most of us still listen to that still, small voice that says, "Not a good idea!"

At the same time, there is not a parent on this earth who has not "lost it" at some point in his or her life—and usually parents have "lost it" in front of their children. So how do we explain self-control to a six-year-old (or a seventeen-year-old) who responds with, "What do you mean, I can always choose to control myself? You don't always control *yourself*!"

My favorite way to illustrate the fact that we choose our feelings (versus other people or things "making" us feel a certain way) is to offer this anecdote:

Your teacher says it is very important that she meet with you after school. You had an activity planned with your friends. Now you will have to miss out on the activity.

You show up at the appointed time. Your teacher is not there yet, so you sit down to wait. While you are waiting, you think about all the fun your friends are having right now. You are upset to be missing out on it.

After a half an hour, your teacher still has not come. You are getting angrier and angrier. "How rude!" you think. "Who does she think she is, making me miss out on having fun with my friends while she doesn't even have the good manners to show up on time!"

After an hour has gone by, you are so mad that you are steaming. "As soon as that teacher shows up, I'm going to really tell her off!" you say to yourself. "I have never been so mad in my life!"

Just then, the principal comes walking up. "What are you doing here?" he asks.

"Waiting for Miss Hopkins," you reply, in a grumbly voice.

"Oh, I'm sorry," the principal replies. "Miss Hopkins was running an errand during her free period and was struck by a hit-and-run-driver. She's in critical condition at the hospital. I've just come to get her lesson plans for the substitute."

At this point, I usually ask the person I'm telling the story to how he or she would then feel if he or she was the student in question. The person's response usually includes sad, worried, concerned, shaken. "But what about angry?" I ask. "Don't you feel angry?"

"Well, *no*," they say, looking at me as if I'm some kind of idiot. "Why would I be angry? It wasn't the teacher's fault she got hit by a car."

"But that doesn't change the fact that you still had to sit there for an hour, and you still missed out on doing stuff with your friends," I argue. "You were angry before you knew what happened. Why aren't you angry now?"

Eventually, the person I'm talking to gets the point I'm trying to make. We do choose how we react to circumstances. Certainly, those circumstances can have an influence on us, but in the end we are in the driver's seat of our emotions. We just don't like to admit to that fact, because it's easier to blame our bad behavior on someone or something else.

Sports, more than almost anything else, should be about self-control—not lack of it. Athletes exhibit self-control every time they harness their muscles to do one more set of push-ups, every time they push themselves to overcome exhaustion to finish one more race.

At the same time, sport is a place where it is extremely easy to lose control because one's emotions are heightened and very close to the surface. It is easy to get carried away without meaning to.

It is important to teach your children that self-control doesn't mean they can't feel upset when they lose a game. Losing hurts.

It's also okay to feel angry when a referee makes a bad call or an opponent says something derogatory. But it is not okay to act on that anger in a way that could be harmful to themselves or others. Instead, they should try such cooling-off techniques as walking away (when possible), taking deep breaths, or talking to the person with whom they feel angry.

During my sophomore year at Stanford, I remember learning from one of my teammates how to express my feelings of frustration and anger when I made a poor play during a basketball game. Oleg Suzdaleff was a crafty senior guard who understood the importance of relieving your feelings and getting right back into the game. When he would make a mistake or get upset about something, he would simply pound one fist into the other, and that ended it.

Oleg also helped me recognize the importance of setting an example for others. When it comes to teaching young people about sportsmanship, adults must set the example. It sounds easy enough—after all, we're the adults—but as many of my previous examples have shown, we are having just as hard a time with self-control as the kids are. Too many of us still have the idea that managing anger means "letting it all out." However, as Cornelia Maude Spelman notes in her book, *When I Feel Angry*, "simply expressing anger without knowing how to reduce and resolve it can lead to its escalation and to violence in words and deeds."[11] When Thomas Junta expressed his anger to Michael Costin over their sons' rough play and Costin supposedly replied something to the effect of, "Hey, that's the way hockey is," they became a textbook example of how expressing anger without trying to reduce and resolve it can lead to violence.

So when your children catch you losing control and call you on it, the first thing you should do is thank them for reminding you that you could be acting better. Point out that just because you're an adult doesn't mean you always act the right way or make the right choices—you're still learning, too. Talk to your children to see if you can determine which one of your "hot buttons" was pushed, and ask for their suggestions on how you might avoid the same thing happening again. Let them actively see you making mistakes and trying to learn from those mistakes. This will encourage them to believe that they can do the same.

Learning from the Experience

The taste of defeat has a richness of experience all its own.

—BILL BRADLEY[12]

At a Wisconsin State Athletic Director's conference that I spoke at a couple of years ago, one of the other speakers related the story of a high school football game that came down to one final play. The score was 7–6. The team that was trailing had the ball. The quarterback lofted a pass and the crowd roared as the receiver caught it for the winning touchdown. As the score of 12–7 was posted on the board, the coach of the winning team pointed out to the officials something they had missed: the receiver had stepped out of bounds before he caught the ball. The scoreboard was changed back to 7–6. Thanks to one brave coach who wasn't afraid to lose, his team's win was now a loss.

John Thompson, former Georgetown basketball coach, once said after a tough loss, "A few losses are good for the soul. You need a few bruises." The awkward thing about losing is that no one is quite sure how a player is supposed to act after a loss. We often tell our children not to cry after losing a game because they're supposed to be "good sports," but it doesn't seem quite right to walk off the field laughing, either.

Since every player will lose sometime, we need to help children prepare themselves in advance for those times when the inevitable happens. We need to explain to them that the best thing to do when they lose isn't to cry or to laugh; the best thing to do is to *think*. Crying over a game won't make a child play any better next time, and neither will laughing. Thinking, however, is always valuable.

Questions to think about after a loss include:

- Did I give it my best effort?
- Was I as mentally and physically prepared as I could have been?
- Was I fully tuned-in to the game at all times?
- How could I have helped prevent the loss?
- How could I have been of more help to my teammates?
- What did the other team do that worked well?
- What would I do differently if I could do it over again?

Teaching your children to ask themselves questions like this is far better than letting them blame the officials, the coach, or the other team for their loss. Of course, hitting them with these questions as soon as they step off the field after a 56–0 loss is not a good idea. Remember, your role as a parent is to support and guide—not lecture and preach.

I recommend first acknowledging your child's feelings of hurt and disappointment, and second asking if the two of you could get together when he or she isn't feeling quite so bad to talk about what happened. That is when you can point out that good players think after every competition—win or lose. That's how they learn not to lose so often.

I wonder what thoughts must have gone through the minds of the young football players whose coach turned their glorious win into a heartbreaking loss. I imagine more than one of them was thinking, "If only he hadn't seen our guy step out of bounds!" or, "Why couldn't he have just kept his mouth shut!"

But hopefully more of the players were thinking about the lessons they learned that day—lessons in honesty, morality, leadership, and sportsmanship. By understanding and valuing those lessons and incorporating them into their lives on and off the playing field, those "losing" players could ensure that their loss was, in the long run, a valuable win.

In her book *Champions Are Raised, Not Born*, Summer Sanders shares a story about how Dot Richardson, a member of the first women's softball team to win an Olympic gold medal, learned early in her childhood the value of learning from a loss:

> "On the way home, in the car, I'm bawling my eyes out," says Dot, "and my dad says to me, 'What are you crying for?'
>
> "'You saw it! I lost the game for us!' I cried. My dad shook his head. 'Listen,' he told me. 'When you're on the field, you do it or you don't. Tonight, you just didn't do it. But you won't let it happen again. You'll practice harder.'"
>
> Dot realized he was right. "I realized at that moment I was going to work harder so it never happened again," she recalls.[13]

Sanders also relates the story of Jeremy, who was a great swimmer in practice but had difficulty dealing with the pressure of a meet:

> Jeremy's parents certainly didn't see any inherent good in failure, and so, I suspect, their attitude infected Jeremy. He came to see losing as something out of his control, something, therefore, totally terrifying. . . . Yet, even the kids with the most talent must learn how to bounce back from failure, because it's part of competition. . . .
>
> When I did lose, I understood it happened for a reason. Defeat meant I hadn't had enough experience going into the race. It never

meant that I was doomed to fail again . . . . Quite the contrary: I was in control. Failure just showed me what, exactly, I had to work on—my stroke, my dive, my turns.[14]

I think two things that make losing hard for people like Jeremy (aside from the usual feelings of embarrassment and humiliation) is that first, losing makes you feel like you're not in control, and second, you don't see the value, or meaning in it.

I can think of no finer example of finding meaning in loss than Lisa Beamer, whose husband, Todd, was on United Flight 93—the only hijacked aircraft on September 11 not to reach its intended target.

Todd Beamer, along with several other passengers, managed to overpower the terrorists and crash the plane before it ended up taking hundreds of innocent lives. In the process, Beamer and the other forty-three passengers on the plane died.

At age thirty-two, Lisa Beamer was a widow, with two little boys and another child on the way. She could have cursed fate. She could have curled up into a ball and railed at how unfair life was— because heaven knows, nothing could have been more unfair than what had happened to her family.

Instead, she decided that the terrorists who took her husband's life would not take hers. She would not let them control her reactions or her actions.

Since her husband's insurance policy had left her provided for, Lisa decided to use the many donations she received after September 11 to start a foundation for the other children who had lost parents on the fateful flight. And when she needed to meet with her husband's former employer to discuss the company's participation in the foundation, she didn't hesitate to fly to San Francisco—on United Flight 93.

"I really wanted to make that meeting and thought, 'I'm not going to let those terrorists affect my life any more than they have,'" Beamer said. "I felt defiant, but I wasn't making any big dramatic statement. I just felt ready to fly again."

Todd Beamer's death wasn't the first tragedy in Lisa's life. When she was fifteen, her father died. It was the perspective she gained from that experience, Beamer noted, that will help her deal with her husband's loss.[15]

By choosing to learn from our bad experiences, we exert control over them. In his book *Real Boys: Rescuing Our Sons from the Myths of Boyhood*, William Pollack, an assistant clinical professor of psychiatry at the Harvard Medical School, shares the story of the Hawks, a group of high school football players from a middle-class suburb of a large northeastern city. The Hawks were not only good football players, but many of them were excellent students, too. One day the Hawks went up against a tough inner-city team. Before the game, the Hawks' coach talked to them about winning and losing. He explained that the opposing team came from a school that didn't have a lot of money, so he didn't want to hear any of his boys teasing the other team about how they looked. He also said that if the Hawks lost, they weren't to say anything bad to the other side—"just shake hands with them and tell them that they played great."

Well, the Hawks went on to lose, badly. And when the game was over, they offered their congratulations to the other team. But they didn't leave it at that. Deciding they could learn from the experience, the Hawks asked their coach if they could do Saturday scrimmages with the other team so that they could improve their skills. As friendships developed, some of the Hawks players began helping boys on the other team with their college admission essays.

Pollack writes, "good sports are about learning from loss, especially about the recognition of limits. . . . As Phillip Isenberg, Harvard Medical School psychiatrist and former Harvard football-team captain, has pointed out, sports teach people that they have to live within the limits of the game and of their bodies, to realize their *relative* talents. No matter what one's skill level, there's almost always someone stronger, faster, or better coordinated. No matter how hard one tries to win, there's also the role of change—the injured star player, the distracting fan, the wind that carries the ball. And no matter how unfair, losing is simply reality."[16]

Losing is never as much fun as winning. However, a true loser is one who yells, cheats, hollers, sulks, and refuses to think, "How can I play better next time?" or, "I played my best, therefore my opponent must have played better than I was today." How your children handle a loss will determine whether or not they are true losers. Successful individuals find positives in failure. Mistakes provide them with information on what needs improvement. So instead of letting your children dwell on their mistakes, help them draw lessons from them for the future.

Letting it go, however, is easier said than done. Not everyone has the maturity, self-confidence, or self-discipline to forget a loss quickly. In an article adapted from his book *Values of the Game*, former U.S. Senator Bill Bradley talks about how difficult it was for him to learn how to cope with defeat as a basketball player. He said the defeat would hang over him "like a fog" for days. It wasn't until his second season in the NBA that he finally received the advice that would help him change his attitude. After losing a close game on a bad pass that he had made, Bradley was dejected. Then Dave DeBusschere, his roommate, set him straight: "You can't go through a season like this. There are too many games. Sure, you blew it tonight, but when it's over, it's over. Let it go. Otherwise you won't be ready to play tomorrow night."

As Bradley said, "I realized that the more you carry the bad past around with you in the present, the less likely it is that the future will improve."[17]

The funny thing is, it might be easier for your kids to teach you about letting go than it is for you to teach them. I remember when I was coaching my youngest son's youth basketball team. We were playing in a big tournament where the winner would advance to the championship game. We ended up losing a close, hard-fought contest. As we were driving home I decided I should say something profound to my son, Peter. After all, I was a psychologist and knew a lot about sports and therefore had a lot of wisdom to share (I thought).

"You know, Peter," I began, "fifty percent of the teams that play basketball lose." No response from Peter. I tried a second time. "*Fifty* percent," I emphasized. Still no reaction. So I resorted to the time-tested method of reaching back into my own childhood. "I remember when I was your age I played in a game that I really wanted to win, and it was really tough when we lost." At that point Peter reached out, gently put his hand on my shoulder and said, "It's okay, Dad."

Children have a wonderful resiliency that adults often lack (either that, or they just have an awfully short attention span). After all, how many times have you watched one of your children come stomping through the front door, saying "I will never play with so-and-so again as long as I live"—only to watch that same child a half-hour later rush out to play with the same friend that only a few minutes earlier was his or her sworn enemy?

We adults, on the other hand, tend to nurse our grudges a little longer. Look at what happened to poor Bill Buckner. He let a baseball slip through his legs, costing the Boston Red Sox a World Series. The last time the Red Sox had won was in 1918. Who knew when their next chance would come? Despite his momentous gaffe, Buckner chose to remain in the Boston area after his retirement from pro ball. Eventually, however, he had to move. Why? Because in seven years, no one let him forget the loss. Fans would still come up to him and make unkind comments. Buckner decided he didn't want his kids hearing about it all the time, so the family finally packed up and left. All because some people just couldn't let it go.

What does it take to be able to let go of a loss and move on?

• **Recognize and accept that some things are beyond your control.** Despite the fact that I have been playing competitive sports for close to six decades, there are still times when I have difficulty in "letting it go." For instance, about a year and a half ago, I took up the sport of racquetball. One of my opponents—a veteran of more than fifty-five years at the game—beats me consistently. This doesn't bother me, but when I play another one of my regular opponents—a young man many years my junior—I can really feel my sportsmanship being put to the test when *he* wins. I think it's because I recognize that with my former opponent, it's his experience that is beating me. I know that experience is something that I can control. If I continue to practice and play racquetball, I, too, will become more experienced. But with my other opponent, it is his youth that is beating me, and there's nothing I can do about that. I certainly can't turn back the clock and make my sixty-something legs act like they did at twenty. Aging is something that is out of my control.

Thus, one of the keys to letting go is recognizing the difference between those things that you can control and those that you can't. As Reinhold Neibuhr wrote in his famous "Serenity Prayer":

God, grant me the serenity
to accept the things I cannot change,
the courage to change the things I can
and the wisdom to know the difference.

• **Understand that sport is about striving to minimize your mistakes, not about trying to be perfect.** Unless you bowl a 300, it is rare that you will ever experience a perfect game in any sport.

The older I get, the more I realize that what sport is about—and what life is about—is trying to make fewer mistakes than we did the day before. There is no room for perfectionism in sport.

Now, a lot of athletes might disagree with me on that—especially the elite ones. Some people take the view that if you're not striving for perfection, then you're not setting your goals high enough. But it is my feeling that those athletes who think they need to be perfect are the ones who will have the hardest time letting go. The pressure they put upon themselves will not only make it hard for them to deal with losses in a sportsmanlike way, but it will also take a lot of the joy out of their sports experience.

So if you see signs of perfectionism in your children, don't make the mistake of seeing it as a good thing. Certainly don't encourage it. Rather, help your children understand that everyone makes mistakes. Mistakes are okay. Mistakes are healthy. And you will love them no matter what mistakes they make.

• **Remember that it is only a game.** In all the sporting events I watched in the days immediately after September 11, the one phrase I heard over and over again was this: "It's only a game." Athletes repeatedly emphasized that neither winning nor losing seemed to hold the same importance when stacked up against the events of that horrible day.

When Hasim Rahman defied twenty-to-one odds to beat heavyweight champ Lennox Lewis, he became an overnight millionaire. But his father, a former prison chaplain, said, "What difference does it make if he makes millions and millions. . . . If he winds up as a bad father, a bad son, and a bad husband, I'd rather see him give it all up."[18]

Sport has the potential to do tremendous things, but in the end, it is never going to cure cancer. It is never going to eliminate world hunger. It is never going to send an astronaut to the moon. What sport *can* do is lift people's spirits. It can bring people together. At its very best, it can help us put aside hatred and move closer to a shared understanding. But it can only do this if the highest standards of sportsmanship are met.

Athletes who remember this, who do their best to exercise self-control in difficult circumstances, and who look at loss as an opportunity to learn something valuable will find that, no matter what the final score, they will always come out ahead.

Letting It Go

Win or lose we have to forget about what happened yesterday and move on to tomorrow.

—Mike Krzyzewski, *Leading with the Heart*[19]

The quickest way to get over a failure is to look in the mirror and admit you had a bad game. That way you start the recovery period that much sooner. That gets me mentally prepared for the next time. I'm never looking at yesterday and seeing how bad I played. I'm looking forward to tomorrow to see how good I can play.

—Michael Jordan[20]

Your children can lose a game and valiantly shake the winner's hand, and they can evaluate their performance after a loss to figure out what they did wrong, but doing all that doesn't guarantee that losing won't still eat away at them. In order to really know how to lose, you have to teach them how to let go of a loss.

MODEL—TEACH—ENCOURAGE

1. Discuss with your children *in advance* what they will do if they lose.
2. Remind your children to always participate in the traditional postgame handshake. Let them know that when

they do this, they are setting a positive tone for players and fans.

3. Find stories in the newspaper where athletes and/or coaches talk about their opponents in a positive way. Contrast these with stories where athletes and/or coaches criticize or demean their opponents. Ask your children who they think sets a better example of sportsmanship, and why?

4. Encourage your children to give credit to their opponent. They need to remember that sometimes the opponent just plays better, or the other coach does a better job.

5. Do not allow your children to blame a loss on injuries or officials. Over the long haul, these variables always seem to even out among opponents.

6. Teach your children that no matter how frustrated or upset they might be becoming during the course of a competition, they should never give in to the temptation to take a cheap shot at an opponent. They should not let bad behavior on the part of others provoke them into equally bad behavior.

7. Help your children recognize the consequences to losing control. (Golfer Matt Kuchar says that as a youngster, he once threw his clubs in a lake. His father made him jump in and fish them out.) Discuss other consequences of losing control with your children, such as incurring a penalty that handicaps the team.

8. Don't ridicule or yell at your children for making a mistake or for losing a game. Instead, say "Even the best players make mistakes. I know you'll do better next time."

9. Help your children understand that controlling their temper is a sign of mental toughness. Point out athletes you notice who keep their cool during trying circumstances.

10. To help your children handle stress better, emphasize effort and improvement, not winning.

11. Let your children see you making mistakes, forgiving yourself, and moving on.
12. Reinforce positive behavior by catching your children exercising self-control and rewarding them for successfully managing their emotions.
13. Enforce your own standards of behavior with your children. Just because their coach might allow them to throw their racket or helmet when they're upset doesn't mean you have to.
14. Help your children exercise self-control by expressing their feelings in ways that are not harmful to themselves or others. Help them determine, in advance, a cooling-off technique to use when they feel angry. This might include counting to ten, taking a deep breath, or thinking of a nonsense word to say (instead of using offensive language).
15. Help your children recognize their "hot buttons." This will make it easier for them to know when to use their cooling-off techniques.
16. Encourage your children not to stew over a loss, but to evaluate it for how they can do better next time.
17. Help your children learn how to accept a loss and move on to the next challenge. Ways to do this include allowing a set amount of time to feel bad (such as twenty minutes or half an hour) and then not letting yourself think about it; writing your feelings down in a letter or journal and then putting it away; talking about how you feel with a parent or friend; making a list of things you can do to be better prepared for the next competition.
18. Help your children put sports in perspective. Make sure their lives (or your family's life) don't revolve around sports, or a loss will take on greater significance. Remind your children that it is only a game—and show by your actions and words that you believe this, too.

19. Focus on fun, not scores. Make a habit after each competition to point out all the positive things that happened (e.g., the weather was great, the team made fewer errors, the parents learned a silly cheer, etc.).

20. Just as you probably have a special ritual for winning, create a special ritual for losing. (Perhaps winning means pizza and losing means root beer floats, or something like that.)

21. Don't try to shield your children from failure or loss. If they get the impression from you that loss is something to be avoided at all costs, as opposed to something to learn and grow from, then they will have a harder time dealing with it successfully.

A Good Sport Understands the Difference Between Winning and Success

I don't agree with the people who say that if I don't hit 40 or 50 or 60 again, I won't have had a great year.

—SAMMY SOSA, AFTER HITTING SIXTY-SIX HOME RUNS
DURING THE 1998 SEASON[1]

In a championship game between two high school soccer teams, one team's goalkeeper was inadvertently kicked and knocked unconscious. With the ball in play and the unfortunate team trying to defend without a goalkeeper, a member of the opposing team intentionally kicked the ball out of bounds to stop play. When asked later why he kicked the ball out of bounds instead of trying to shoot it into the open goal, the young man said, "If someone is hurt like that, especially the goalie, you do that [kick it out]. If I had scored, it's not much of a goal."[2]

This young soccer player understood the difference between winning and success—that one does not necessarily equal the other. Not everyone recognizes that difference. As the coaching education consultant for the Anaheim Union High School District, I work with approximately 150 to 175 new coaches every year, trying to prepare them to meet the challenges of coaching in the twenty-first century. One of the issues we continually struggle with is what constitutes a successful season? Can you have a winning season without necessarily having a successful season, and vice versa?

Most of these coaches, like many other people out there, believe that if you win at sports, you can be considered successful, and that you can't be considered successful unless you win.

But I disagree. A friend of mine, sociologist Marty Miller, explains it this way:

> Winning and success are not synonymous. Neither success nor failure depends on the ball game's outcome or the won and lost record. Success is effort, good feeling, comradeship, making a contribution, gaining skills, and having fun—things we have some control over. . . . Individuals have control over the amount of effort they put forth in a game, but they have limited control over the final points on the scoreboard. Success is what youngsters strive for, but winning is what adults value, and kids know it.[3]

As I work with my group of young coaches (most of whom are still in school), I try to do whatever it takes—plead, cajole, challenge—to get them to realize that success is things like effort, accomplishment, being with friends, making a contribution, gaining skills, and enjoying oneself. I want them to understand these things before it is too late. I want them to understand it before they start losing games and championships and feel the same sense of failure and loss of self-worth that I did when I played. I want them to understand it before they start passing the wrong attitude on to their players.

It is when athletes equate winning with success (and vice versa) that sportsmanship problems often arise. And no wonder! If you have to win in order to feel successful, then losing becomes an even bigger blow to the ego than it already is. The pressure to win—and maintain one's self-esteem and status in the sports world—becomes even greater. Unless an athlete is thoroughly grounded in the basic elements of sportsmanship, the temptation to cheat, bend the rules, or throw a fit when things aren't going well will be difficult to overcome.

So how do you help your kids recognize the difference between winning and success? First, you have to examine your own attitudes and beliefs. How important do you feel winning is in the grand scheme of life? I know one mom who thought she was pretty enlightened when it came to sportsmanship issues—until her favorite basketball team experienced its first losing season in about two decades. Suddenly, she couldn't even read the sports pages anymore because it was just too painful. "Oh, great," she thought. "If I'm like this over a bunch of guys I don't even know, what am I going to do when my *kid's* team starts losing?"

One of the greatest examples I've seen recently of adults who truly understand the difference between winning and success came at the 2001 Little League World Series. When the Oceanside American Little League All-Stars lost a heartbreaking game to Bronx, New York, Oceanside team manager Daryl Wasano and league president Glen Mills refrained from criticizing the umpire whose blown call led to the loss. Later, these same two men encouraged parents and fans not to be bitter when it was learned that the Bronx team's star pitcher was actually an ineligible four-teen-year-old player. The Oceanside team may not have won the game, but in their effort and their example they were an unqualified success.

If you really want your children to believe that winning and success are not the same thing, you have to believe it yourself. Only then can you begin to help your children understand that winning is not the most important part of their sports experience, and that true success comes through competing against themselves and enjoying and learning from their sports experience.

Winning—Not the Most Important Thing

A crossword puzzle my wife and I were once working on asked for a five-letter word for "places second." Answer: "loses."
—RUSSELL W. GOUGH, CHARACTER IS EVERYTHING[4]

I've learned a lot since I was a sports parent. I know I wanted my kids to enjoy their sports experiences more than I enjoyed mine, but I also remember the pressure I felt as I watched them compete. Would they win? Would they lose? If they lost, how would they feel? How would I comfort them? (I always assumed losing would be as painful for them as it had been for me.) And I'm sure some of that pressure had to show on my face.

It wasn't until I became a sports grandparent that I really understood that there was a decided difference between winning and success. And once I understood that, a lot of the pressure I felt with sports went away. When I watch my oldest granddaughter at her swim meet, I see the satisfaction she takes in her ability to change strokes with each lap and I sense her pleasure at having her family there to support her. When I watch my five-year-old grandson smack the T-ball and run for first base as if he were competing in the Olympic 100-meter finals, I see someone who is the picture of pure joy. And I finally *get* it. They are having fun. I am having fun. Hence, the experience is an unqualified success.

For his book *Real Boys' Voices*, William Pollack interviewed hundreds of boys from across the country to get their opinions and thoughts on the pressures and challenges that the boys of today's world face. In one particularly striking account, a sixteen-year-old boy named Jake talks about his indoctrination into the "winning is everything" creed:

Ever since I've played Little League the word "win" has been forced into my mind. When I was eight years old, the coach would tell us at the beginning of the season that we were just out there for fun, but I knew that it wasn't true. Every day that there was a game, my day would be ruined. I was too worried to go anywhere and was constantly thinking about the game. I envied my friends who didn't play baseball and wished that I could be in their shoes. You could always see the disappointment in the eyes of the coaches— one of whom was my father—when we lost, and you could see the delight in their eyes when we won. Now don't get me wrong; I love the game of baseball and because of the coaches' winning mentality we won championships three out of the four years that I was playing. But did I love Little League? No!

After a few years passed, I found a new sport that I loved: soccer. I had played soccer since I was four years old, but I didn't love it as much as baseball until my last year of Little League. . . . I played the sport year-round and was all set for the challenge of high school soccer. Boy, did I get a big surprise. The high school soccer coach was all about winning! He said, "We are only here for one reason, and that is to win. If you are out here to have fun then you should go home now." I had problems my first year playing for this man, and after it was over I wanted to quit. I wasn't having fun in the way that I always had, and I longed to be four years old again, when winning was not our only reason to play. But I decided to stick with soccer and just block out the coach.

There was still that winning mentality through the four years that I was playing, but I did manage to have some fun. I am a little ashamed to say that in the meantime, the mentality has rubbed off on me. Now everything to me is about winning. I believe in winning now, and I can only hope that I don't pass this trait on to my son to the extent that I had it passed on to me.[5]

Where do children pick up the idea that they have to win in order to be successful? As Jake's story illustrates, it usually begins with coaches and/or parents who imply as much—either directly or indirectly—through their looks, their words, and their actions.

For instance, if your child comes home after a game and the first words out of your mouth are "Who won?" or even the seemingly innocent "How'd you do?" the implication is that the main thing you're interested in is results. This doesn't mean that you can't ask those questions, or that you're a bad parent for wondering what the outcome was. Of course you're curious. And of course you hope that your child did well. But if you want to pass on a "winning isn't everything" attitude to your children, you need to train yourself to put the emphasis on fun and process by making sure your first questions are along the lines of "Did you have fun?" or "What things did you learn today?"

Emphasizing process over results can be a challenging thing to do, because that's not how most of the adult world functions. How often do we hear an employer say, "Look, I don't care how you do it—just get it done!" What are we told to emphasize on our résumés? Results. "Landed $5 million account." "Generated over $200,000 in sales." "Supervised forty-two employees." Even our annual Christmas newsletters tend to focus heavily on accomplishments: "Janie got straight A's for the third year in a row, while Billie was elected class president and cocaptain of his varsity basketball team."

So when parents and coaches find themselves kicking the bleachers after a loss, it is often a reflection of society's attitude toward winning. After all, don't you remember what the tag line was for the Nike ad campaign during the Centennial Olympic Games? "You don't win silver, you lose gold."

As Americans, we are an extremely competitive society, and we learn this competitiveness at a very early age. It is not unusual for my eight- and ten-year-old granddaughters to have anywhere from three to five hours of homework per night, and there is always some concern (either spoken or unspoken) as to how they're doing scholastically, both on the part of the girls and their parents. Are they keeping up? Are they acing their tests? How do they measure up against their classmates?

Parents feel enormous pressure to make sure their children can survive in today's competitive world. This causes them to feel the need to begin teaching their children at younger and younger ages. This is probably best exemplified by parents who strap headphones onto the bulging belly of the expectant mother, in the hopes that their unborn child will develop an appreciation of classical music while in the womb. But it is also seen in parents who haul their three-year-olds out to the golf course or the tennis courts in the hopes that early training will produce the next Tiger Woods or Venus Williams. Not only does this put a lot of pressure on kids, but it also takes away from them the opportunity to learn and make choices for themselves.

Winning, being the best, being number one, has become our narcotic. It has become an obsession. And as such, it is responsible for much of the dysfunctional behavior of today's athletes, including the need for constant external recognition, the focus on perfection, the habit of blaming others when things go wrong, and the tendency to measure one's self-worth solely on the outcome of one's performance.

At the same time, I don't necessarily agree with the people who feel that competitiveness is bad, and that winning shouldn't be a consideration in sports at all. To try to promote the "fun and learning" aspect of sports, some people have instituted "scoreless" games where children just play for a designated amount of time and then the game is over.

I don't think that it's bad to be competitive, and I don't think we need to eliminate the process of keeping score from our athletic competitions. I just think we need to expand our definition of winning to recognize that the score doesn't always define a true winner. Winners are also people who give their best effort and who continue to learn and improve.

At one basketball camp I participated in, I was struck by how many times the director of the program (Herb Livsey, a veteran basketball man from Southern California who spends most of his time as a scout for the Portland Trail Blazers) emphasized that the goal of each athlete ought to be on improvement—not on making all-league, getting a scholarship, or playing professional ball. As Herb repeatedly stated, everyone could improve. It was a goal they could all achieve.

I really had the self-improvement lesson brought home to me a few years ago after I had undergone two heart procedures and surgery for cancer. The doctors said I had to get more exercise, so I dutifully packed myself off to the gym, hating every minute of it. Then a friend asked me to play on his seniors basketball team. Even though it had been more than forty years since I had played basketball regularly, I think some little part of me still expected that I could step onto the court and have everything come right back. As it was, it took a year for my jump shot to return and another year before I could comfortably drive to either side of the basket and throw up a hanging hook shot. To this day, I continue to improve my game, and that makes it enjoyable and fun for me.

When we focus as much (or more) attention on effort, improvement, and enjoyment as we do on winning, *then* we redefine what it means to be a winner, and help our children understand the true meaning of success.

Competing Against Yourself

Don't measure yourself by what you've accomplished, but rather by what you should have accomplished with your abilities.

—JOHN WOODEN[6]

Steffi Graf, one of the world's greatest tennis players, always said she didn't play for records. When she won the Golden Slam in 1988 (all four major titles and the Olympics), Graf said the accomplishment itself wasn't that important to her. What was important was playing her best, and making her best better every year.

In sports, the word "success" is usually used to describe a desired outcome or goal. A *successful* athlete is someone who performs at a certain established level. There are two ways of measuring this success. The first is to use objective standards, the most common of which is who gets the most points. When this standard is used to measure performance, success is based on outcome. However, since so few make it to the top in athletics, outcome (who wins) is not the best way of determining success. Therefore, it is better for parents, athletes, and coaches to define success on the basis of self-improvement.[7]

This self-improvement can take many forms. The most obvious is improvement in performance. But athletes can also improve in their attitudes (being open to learning, being more positive) and their behaviors (showing up for practice on time, becoming more of a team player, etc.).

How can you as a parent help your children recognize and measure their own improvement?

• Make sure your motives are pure. If you're pushing self-improvement because *you* are the one who's not satisfied with your child's performance, then you need to step back and ask yourself, "Why is it so important to me that my child do well in sports?" I remember observing a group of parents watching their six-year-olds participate in the first few practices of an instructional basketball league. As one little boy bobbled a pass, his father leaned over and said to the dad sitting next to him, "I know he can do better than that. We've been practicing this at home." Meanwhile, the second dad could not have cared less about the performance of the boy in question, because he was too busy agonizing over his own son's bobbled passes.

• Help your children identify where they are and where they want to be in terms of improvement. This could take the form of just sitting down and talking with them about it, or helping them create a chart or some other written form of measurement. Be sure to let your children decide how they want to keep track of their improvement. As always, your role as parent is to be a sounding board and to provide advice or suggestions only when your children give you permission to do so.

• Look for signs of improvement in your children and point them out with specific, not general or vague, comments. For example, saying, "Stacie, I noticed you didn't pout today after you struck out—way to go!" is better than, "I noticed you had a better attitude today, Stacie."

- Remind them always to measure themselves against them-selves, not against others. I've worked with many accomplished NBA athletes over the years, and one thing I've noticed is that they don't sit around poring over the newspaper to see who is out-rebounding whom. Their main focus is always on improving their own performances from practice to practice and game to game.

When "winning" depends on improving or exceeding personal and team performance and striving for excellence, then everyone has the opportunity to be a winner. Beating an opponent is excit-ing, but performing to your personal best is real success.

Here's an example of this that you may be able to relate to. A couple of years ago, a friend of mine ran in her first 10k race. Out of 103 runners in her age category, she finished ninety-first. How-ever, she was as happy as if she had finished first. Why? Because she knew that for her, simply finishing the run was a personal best. You see, as a child she had never been very athletic. She couldn't throw a ball. She couldn't run very fast. She was always picked last for any team. As she told me, "I loved sports—as a spectator. But when it came to participating, sports were the bane of my exis-tence. If there had been a category in our yearbook for 'Most Likely to Finish a 10K in Their Forties,' you certainly wouldn't have seen my name in it. That's why it felt so wonderful to actu-ally run a race! I know I'll never be one of the top finishers, but that's not what I'm out there for. Just the fact that I *am* out there, as opposed to sitting on my couch watching TV, means I've already won."

When your only goal is to beat another competitor, you're in trouble. That's because you have no control over other people. You can't control whether the officials are going to make bad calls or good calls. You can't control whether a teammate is going to be on top of his or her game or in a funk over not having a date to the prom. You can't control whether your opponent is going to be fired up or apathetic. My friend the 10K runner didn't feel successful because she beat other runners; she felt successful because she achieved a personal goal. She felt successful because her definition of success didn't mean winning the race—it meant finishing the race.

In Murrieta, California, there is a residential facility for students ranging in age from eleven to eighteen who have problems that interfere with their ability to be educated in a regular school setting. Students at the facility, Oak Grove Institute, are usually placed in therapy programs that run from nine to fifteen months. Once they complete their programs, they return to their regular schools.

In 1998, Oak Grove's physical education teacher started a girl's basketball team that he hoped would help teach these troubled young women about life. It was a chance for the girls to have something "normal" in their lives, and to interact with other kids in a normal setting. The only problem was, they totally stunk at playing basketball. Most of the girls had never seen a basketball game before. They didn't even have a real court of their own to practice on. Instead, they used a converted tennis court. In one infamous game, the Oak Grove Monarchs scored a whopping two points—while the other team scored seventy-eight.

Now, if this were a movie, the Monarchs would work hard and overcome numerous challenges to pull off an astounding win over a highly ranked rival. But Oak Grove isn't a movie. It's real life. The Monarchs did work hard. They did overcome challenges. But they never even came close to winning a game. However, as they played, something interesting began happening. Members of the opposing crowds started to take it upon themselves to cheer for the Monarchs, whose own parents usually were unable to attend games. Referees would stop calling every foul (and believe me, there were a lot of them to call) and instead offer advice to the Monarchs' coach.

Despite the outcomes of their games, these girls began to see themselves as winners. For the first time in their lives, they had stuck with something no matter how hard it got. For the first time, they felt like they belonged to something. For the first time, they had people cheering *for* them, instead of against them.[8]

Hopefully, they will be able to use these feelings to tackle other challenges in their lives. Because once we change our definition of success, it liberates us to take on new goals. I remember clearly the summer after my junior year in college, I was so buoyed by my success in meeting my goals on the basketball court that I decided to take piano lessons—something I never would have dreamed of doing before. But I had gained a self-confidence that I hadn't previously had, and this allowed me to feel that even if I didn't become the next Van Cliburn, it was okay. I didn't have to be a virtuoso to make the experience worthwhile.

These examples illustrate the importance of measuring yourself against your own yardstick, rather than those that are provided by the accomplishments or expectations of others. Some concrete ways you can help your children do this include the following:

• Never compare your children to anyone else. They will do enough of this on their own. Your job is to help your children recognize their individual worth and the things that make them unique.

• Remind your children to work toward skill improvement and good sportsmanship in every game. And of the two, I would put the emphasis on good sportsmanship. Why? Because sometimes kids aren't going to be able to improve their skills. Sometimes they will have an off game, or feel tired or stressed or unwell, and this will affect their physical performance. But sportsmanship can always be improved. They can always offer a little extra encouragement to a teammate, or congratulate their opponent with a little more sincerity. In fact, those times when their skills are being most tested are often the times when they can make the greatest improvement in their sportsmanship.

• Help your children set reasonable, achievable goals for measuring success. Too many times kids will set unreachable goals and then get frustrated because they can't meet them. You may need to talk to your children about how to set reasonable goals, and give them examples of what some reasonable goals might be for their age and skill level (if you don't know what these would be, then get some suggestions from your child's coach). Explain to them the goal-setting process: that a goal consists of a reasonable objective, a method for achieving the objective, and a deadline for achieving it. Share with them some examples of goals that you have set for yourself, and how you met them.

Children who are encouraged to measure themselves in this way will not allow themselves to become overly disheartened or overly puffed up by the message on the scoreboard. They will also be better prepared to deal with the successes and disappointments of life, whether as children or adults.

Learning from the Experience

Your journey is the important thing. A score, a trophy, a ribbon is simply the inn.

—JOHN WOODEN[9]

What is the "journey" of sport? It is the practicing, the learning, the satisfaction of working to accomplish goals, the excitement of putting on a uniform, the richness of friendships made and expanded, the pleasure of smelling the grass or hearing the smack of the ball against the wooden floor or the leather mitt. Sometimes it is the sprained ankles, torn muscles, and natural limitations of the human body. Overall, it is every moment—the good and the bad—of the entire sports experience. Athletes who are able to focus on and appreciate the journey of their sports experience will get more from it than any amount of trophies or awards could ever offer.

Summer Sanders has said that the Olympics never were her destination. She started competitive swimming as a way to hang out with her brother and his friends, and she kept it up because it was fun. That she one day ended up winning a gold medal was simply a "career perk."[10]

Unfortunately, it is a sad trait of human nature that many of us tend to go through life focusing on our destination, not on the journey that gets us there. Sport is no different. When this happens, winning assumes a greater importance, and losing becomes almost unbearable.

I was reminded of this at a recent college reunion when a fraternity brother remarked on how I had "always been worrying about something." He was right. Even though, as a sophomore, I had made first team all-conference and was an honorable mention All-American, I still spent the summer worrying about whether I'd make first string the next season. Such insecurity and fear of failure kept me from truly enjoying the game and the friendships I had with my teammates. I spent my time hurrying to practice, hurrying to class, hurrying to the library, and so on, instead of developing relationships and taking time to participate in the whole college experience. It is something I intensely regret to this day.

Russell Gough shares a similar message with the story of a friend of his, Olympic water polo player Terry Schroeder. After losing to Spain in the semifinals of the 1992 Barcelona Games, Schroeder and his wife were on their way back to the Olympic village. Since Barcelona would be his last Olympics, Schroeder was feeling angry and frustrated at the fact that he would never win the gold medal that he so anxiously sought. Then he ran into another former Olympian—Kirk Kilgour—who had been paralyzed in an accident. Kilgour was driving his wheelchair with his tongue. The encounter changed his whole perspective. As Schroeder said:

> Here I was, whining, moaning, and groaning, feeling totally sorry for myself because I hadn't won a gold medal. And there was Kirk, forever confined to a wheelchair, smiling and happy, being very positive about life. . . .
>
> It became clear to me, then and there, how you can focus so much on winning that it can really affect your character—not to mention the character of those around you. . . . I hate to admit it, but I think at times I let my desire to win a gold medal overshadow the most important things in my life. . . .
>
> It's not ultimately about medals or win-loss records or getting your picture in the sports pages. Winning is important, but it's not *most* important. What's most important are the internal things—personal growth, improving your character, even developing long-lasting friendships.[11]

The Olympic creed says in part "the essential thing is not to have conquered but to have fought well." "Fighting well" is not always something that is easy for young people to do, however. After games at Jefferson High in Los Angeles, Jefferson football coach Hank Johnson has a tradition of having his players line up at the visitors' exit gate and applaud their opponents as they leave the field. Win or lose, Johnson's players are there clapping. After one game, however, in which they lost by thirty points (and their opponent was still trying to run up the score late in the fourth quarter), the players didn't want to clap. Johnson still made them do it. "As [the opposing players] got on their bus and drove away, our kids were crying. I was crying too. But we got all the kids together and I told them we are never going to rub another team's face in it like that if we were beating them that badly. Then, an assistant principal from [the other school] came over and said, 'Coach, may I say something to the team?' I said sure. She said, '[We] beat you guys today, but Jefferson is the real winner here. I've never seen a group of young men with so much class.'"[12]

Of course, stories like these are all very fine and good, but when you get right down to it, how do you get your kids to appreciate and enjoy the "journey" of sport, and not attach so much importance to the destination? Here are some suggestions:

• Begin by setting an example. If you're driving your kids to their game on a perfect fall day, point out your surroundings. Talk about how great it is that they have the opportunity to be outside on a day like this. Share memories of your childhood sports experiences—the smells, the tastes, the sounds. I have one friend for whom the smell of baked potatoes never fails to conjure up memories of sitting in the stands at her high school football games, when there was snow on the ground and foil-wrapped potatoes— hot and steaming from the oven—were used to warm both the hands and the stomach.

• Point out that a common characteristic of successful people is that they don't do something because of the final outcome (a winning score, a big paycheck). They do it because they love what they do. For example, Michael Jordan didn't return to basketball (twice) because he needed the money. He did it because he loves the game.

• Help your children recognize aspects of the journey that they might otherwise overlook. For instance, Coach Johnson realized that part of getting his players to appreciate the journey of sport involved showing appreciation toward their companions on that journey—in other words, their opponents. Sometimes it was a hard thing for his players to do, but I can bet you it was a lesson that will always stand out in their memories.

• Remind your children of what we talked about in the previous chapter—that even when they lose, there is always something they can learn that makes the experience worthwhile. The football players at Jefferson High, for example, learned that sometimes in life we encounter individuals whose sole purpose seems to be to make us miserable. It can be an opponent who runs up the score, an overbearing teacher, an unethical boss, or a backstabbing friend. We can either choose to let these people bring us down to their level, or we can make a conscious effort to rise above it. And when we rise above it, we serve as an example to others.

In sum, understanding the difference between winning and success means:

• Recognizing that a winner isn't necessarily the person or team with the most points, but rather is someone who gives maximum effort, and who continues to learn and improve.
• Not comparing yourself to others, but defining success on the basis of personal improvement.
• Enjoying the "journey" of sports—the friendships, the satisfaction of improving one's skills, the excitement of competition, and all the other little things that make sports fun.

Athletes who understand the difference between winning and success will find that they have the opportunity to be successful every time they step onto the athletic field. This knowledge will enable them to have a sense of self-esteem and self-control that will help them exhibit the behavior of "good sports."

MODEL—TEACH—ENCOURAGE

1. Remind your children (and yourself) that the overriding reason why they should participate in sports is for the fun of it. If they're not having fun, then you need to talk to them to find out if it's just a temporary feeling (perhaps due to a poor performance) or a more long-term problem. Be supportive of their feelings and let them know you'll support whatever decision they make about their sports career.
2. Do not allow your children to tease or make fun of people who lose. For younger children, there are many good books at the library that deal with teaching children empathy for others. With older children, I have found that involving them in service projects is an excellent way to teach them empathy.
3. Teach your children that hard work and an honest effort are often more important than a victory.
4. Help your children work toward skill improvement and good sportsmanship in every game.
5. Teach your children how to set reasonable and achievable self-improvement goals.
6. Adopt self-improvement as a standard for success in your family.

7. Avoid placing unrealistic expectations on your children.
8. Avoid using an older brother's or sister's performance as a standard for success (such as expecting a child to make first-string because his or her sibling did).
9. Compliment your children on their improvement. Younger children should receive these verbal rewards frequently and generously. Older children and adolescents, on the other hand, should be praised only when their performance merits it (they will know if you are being insincere or fishing for positive things to say). Avoid dishonesty, such as saying "You played well today" if a child didn't.
10. Remind your children that most successful people do what they do because they love it, not because they're looking for a big payoff.
11. Help your children keep sports in perspective. After speed skater Dan Jansen placed a disappointing second in his first national championship, he cried all the way home. Then his dad reminded him, "Dan, there's more to life than skating around in a circle."[13] Again, service projects are an excellent way for children to see that there are things that are more important than sports.
12. Work with your children to establish a set of family sports values outlining those things your family considers an important part of a successful sports experience. (These may include such things as fair play, a good effort, positive interactions with others, etc.) Write them down and refer to these values often.
13. Encourage your children to write personal "mission statements" regarding their sports goals and visions.
14. Encourage your children to base their judgment of whether they were successful, not on whether they won, but on whether they put forth their best effort.

15. Encourage your children to strive for the self-satisfaction of knowing they did their best.
16. Help your children understand that winning is something that is often out of their control. However, playing their best is something that they do have some measure of control over.
17. Discourage envy, jealousy, and criticism in your children. Remind them that these feelings are counterproductive and hurt no one but themselves.

A Good Sport Respects Others

"I hate them."

Reggie Miller didn't hide his feelings Monday as he spoke about the New York Knicks and the Eastern Conference's other great rivalry.

The Pacers' guard stayed away from the "I respect them" line that had cushioned his remarks a day earlier.

"They always think they're bigger and badder than everyone," Miller said. "And we know they don't give us any respect. So why should I give respect or like someone that doesn't give us respect?"

—"MILLER SAYS HE HATES KNICKS," DESERET NEWS, MAY 23, 2000[1]

Respect is a quality that sometimes seems at odds with the chest-thumping bravado of athletic competition. Athletes are taught to view opponents as "the enemy." Fans yell, "Kill the ump!" A coach who loses a critical game wakes up to find that unforgiving followers have placed "for sale" signs on his front lawn.

Teaching children to respect their compatriots in sports can be a major task, especially when the actions of others (most notably, professional athletes) sometimes give little cause for respect.

The quandary faced by a friend of mine—a big Utah Jazz fan—illustrates this issue. After the Jazz were ousted from the NBA 2000 playoffs by the Portland Trail Blazers (and the Miami Heat met a similar fate at the hands of the New York Knicks), the stage was for the Trail Blazers and the Los Angeles Lakers to meet in the Western Conference final and the Knicks and the Indiana Pacers to bump heads in the East. After one look at this mix of big egos, big tempers, and big trash talkers, my friend complained to a local sports columnist:

> Dear Brad Rock:
> I had to chuckle when I read your question in yesterday's column, "Is anyone having a hard time deciding who to cheer for— Shaq or Rasheed?" I had just finished writing a letter to my mother bemoaning Miami's loss to New York, explaining that my husband and I had been rooting for Miami as the "lesser of two evils."
> The saddest thing about the departure of the Jazz from the playoffs is that there are no good guys left to cheer for. At least last year we could feel good about San Antonio winning, but who among the current crop of finalists can give us that same feeling? I had decided to cast my vote for Indiana until reading Reggie "I Hate Them" Miller's little diatribe in the paper. Now we have plenty of good athletes to choose from, but not a single good sport. Am I the only one who thinks this is wrong?

Such recent events in our country's history as the September 11 tragedy and the shooting at Columbine High School show that the need to help children learn respect for others has seldom been greater. To this end, I believe that involving children in such experiences of "community" that sport provides is an invaluable way of helping them learn to care about and be considerate of other people. As Shari Young Kuchenbecker notes in *Raising Winners*, "Sports activities offer children chances to build social as well as physical skills. . . . In a culture where opportunities to learn face-to-face social skills are increasingly limited, quality social learning in athletic situations becomes all the more important."[2]

But if sport offers so many opportunities to cultivate respect for others, why don't we see more of it in our athletic competitions? Part of it has to do with the competitive nature of sport. When you're fighting to be number one, respect can be seen as a sign of weakness.

Another reason has to do with how our culture treats athletes. Typically, people become less self-centered and more considerate of others as they grow older. With athletes, that is not always the case. At the root of this problem is the special treatment that athletes often receive. For instance, you've probably heard stories about teachers grading athletes more leniently, or consistently allowing them to turn assignments in late. Parents can fall into the "special treatment" trap as well. Maybe you excuse the athlete in your family from doing chores that his or her siblings have to do. Perhaps your family's schedule revolves around the athlete, or you spend more money on your athletic child than you do on the others.

Athletes who receive this kind of special treatment often start to believe they are different from everyone else. They think this means they don't have to treat other people with respect or consideration. As a parent, you need to carefully guard against letting this happen to your child, especially if he or she is an elite athlete, where the special treatment becomes even more pronounced.

To answer Reggie Miller's question, "Why should you respect someone who doesn't respect you?" I would have to say, because a good sport doesn't sink to someone else's level. A good sport isn't afraid to set the example. A good sport understands that lack of respect for others on the part of athletes undermines the ability of the sports program to provide everyone with a quality experience.

Treating all people with courtesy, kindness, and respect is an essential quality for children to develop. There is nothing that says these qualities need to be set aside when they step onto the sports field.

Defining Respect

Before you can teach your children about respect, you must first understand what it is. Like sportsmanship, respect is one of those things that everyone defines differently. For instance, some parents feel it is disrespectful for their children's friends to address them by their first name. They prefer to be called "Mr." or "Mrs." Other parents would rather be called by their first names and feel a little bit insulted if they're not.

In general, respect means recognizing that a person, situation, or thing has value and acting accordingly. For example, many coaches insist their athletes tuck their jerseys in because they feel being neatly dressed shows respect for the game. In today's casual-to-the-max society, many young players don't understand or agree with this point of view. But if they respect their coach, they will show that they value his or her feelings by tucking in their jerseys.

On the other hand, you will find coaches who really don't care whether their players' jerseys are tucked in or not, or how long their shorts are, or whether they've dyed their hair to match the school colors. As long as the players are doing their jobs and giving 100 percent effort, the coach is satisfied.

This is why it's sometimes hard to teach our kids what respect is—because it's different things to different people. For example, let's take the subject of trash talk, and its close relative, taunting. To me, these things are terribly disrespectful. But not everyone agrees.

During the 1999–2000 basketball season the Los Angeles Clippers were playing the San Antonio Spurs. Before the game began the two teams were amazingly cordial and friendly, hugging each other and so forth. Apparently, the many young players on each team had become acquainted through years of youth basketball and summer camps across the nation.

During the contest, Cuttino Mobley of San Antonio had a career night, including several dunks over much taller players. With each successful effort, he ran by the Clipper bench and celebrated with an in-your-face demonstration. Apparently, no one took offense, because after the game the players were all hugs and smiles again.

Yet just a few years ago, during a playoff game between the Jazz and the Lakers, Jazz reserve player Greg Foster had the Lakers practically foaming at the mouth after he scored a quick basket and ran past the Lakers' bench with a throat-slashing gesture.

This brings up an interesting issue. When is trash talking and taunting considered an acceptable part of the game, and when is it considered an unacceptable display of poor sportsmanship?

In my day, even the act of dunking (not that it was an option for me at five feet, eight inches) was considered taunting, or showboating, and would lead to a benching or at least a severe reprimand by one's coach. Today, players get booed for *not* dunking.

Even the experts cannot agree on whether trash talk and the like are a relatively harmless form of cultural expression or a dangerous indication of the deterioration of sports. In *Coaching for Character*, Clifford and Feezell offer this opinion about trash talking: "There's a point at which good-natured teasing turns into disrespectful taunting and trash talking. It requires an appreciation of the particular sport, the level at which it's being played, and the background of the players to make particular decisions about where to draw this line, but it's a line that true competitors need to draw. When in doubt, keep your mouth shut."[3]

As my son the schoolteacher said to me, if taunting happens on the playground with kids you grew up with, know, and respect, then it's okay. But in situations where players don't know each other, then it's wrong. And to do it with somebody who is not your friend is unsportsmanlike.

Because of the inconsistency in what different athletes, coaches, etc., feel is respectful and disrespectful in sports, I've compiled a list of what I feel are the ten most common ways athletes show disrespect. Hopefully this list will help you as you try to give your children guidelines on what is and isn't respectful in their various sports settings.

Ten Ways Athletes Show Disrespect

1. **Blaming.** Blaming is disrespectful because the person doing it is not accepting responsibility for his or her part in the loss or the missed play. (I talk more about teaching your children responsibility in Chapter Six, "A Good Sport Shows Integrity.")

2. **Complaining.** Complaining is similar to blaming. Often the person doing the complaining is not accepting responsibility for his or her part in the problem. Complaining about a call the official made, or complaining about lack of playing time or being pulled from the game is disrespectful because it shows a lack of respect for the other person's authority. As a coach, I found it hard to have respect for those athletes who complained. The ones I respected were the ones who disagreed with me but kept their mouths shut and quietly went about proving me wrong.

3. **Shaming.** If it's a teammate the athlete is shaming or making fun of, often the purpose is to get that person to play better. ("C'mon, man, you blocked like a *girl* on that last play! You can do better than that!") If you see your children doing this, you need to explain to them that negative motivation seldom works as well as positive motivation. If your children are very young, you may need to give them some examples of positive motivation. If it's an opponent that your child is shaming (trash talk falls into this cat-

egory), the motivation is usually to make the other player feel upset enough to play poorly. However, not only does this often have the opposite effect, it doesn't say much for your child's respect for his or her own skills if he or she has to resort to these kinds of tactics to win.

4. **Showboating.** Showing off (high stepping into the end zone, doing a slam dunk when no one's within ten feet of you, etc.) is not respectful because it belittles your opponent's efforts and focuses all the attention on you. In team sports, it can even show disrespect for your teammates, because without their efforts you probably wouldn't be making that touchdown or basket. As a parent, you can discourage showboating by expressing your disappointment when a child chooses to showboat. If you and your child are watching sports on television, you can refrain from cheering or complimenting the athletes you see showboating.

5. **Discounting.** What does *discounting* mean? Discounting is when an athlete says, "Of course they beat us. We've played three 'away' games in a row. And we lost our star player! I'd like to see anyone play their best under those circumstances!" After the BCS announced (just a few days before the last game of the regular season) that Brigham Young University's undefeated 2001 football team would not be considered for one of the big-name bowl games, the demoralized Cougars got whomped by an unranked Hawaii team. The Cougars could have discounted Hawaii's win by saying, "Well, we had jet lag, and it was hard getting used to the artificial turf, and our leading rusher was out with a broken leg, and then we were sucker-punched by the BCS, so no wonder Hawaii won!" But they didn't do that. "It doesn't do any good to cry and whine about it," said center Jason Scukanec. "You have to take it like a man. You win like a man; you lose like a man. They beat us, and my hat's off to them."

6. **Ignoring.** Ignoring someone else—a teammate, a coach—isn't just rude. It also shows that you're not open to learning from that person. We need to help our children realize that one reason we treat other people with respect is that there is always something we can learn from them. (Granted, sometimes the only thing we can learn is patience in dealing with difficult people. But still, that's a valuable lesson, isn't it?)

7. **Excluding.** To me, the main benefit of team sports is that it teaches young people how to get along with a wide variety of individuals. When athletes either purposely or unconsciously exclude teammates, they are not only showing disrespect to that person, they are failing to learn valuable lessons and skills. If you see your children excluding others, you first need to find out why. Is it because the other person isn't a very good player? Is the other person hard to get along with? Is it because the other person comes from a different background, or is the new person in an already-established group? Second, you need to help your child feel empathy for this person. Remind your child of times when he or she has felt on the "outside." Finally, you may need to help your child develop concrete skills to reach out to the other person (for example, if there's a language barrier, you could teach your child—or better yet, the whole team—a few key phrases in the excluded child's language).

8. **Belittling.** Belittling is kind of a cross between shaming and discounting. In essence, it means making light of someone else's efforts. Athletes who belittle others generally do so because they feel insecure about their own contributions. If you feel that your child is belittling, you need to gently but firmly help the child recognize why he or she is doing this, and help your child come up with some alternative ways of behaving. Here's an example:

Athlete: Angie's such a wuss. Did you see her duck when that ball came sailing into the outfield today? I don't know why she even thinks she can play baseball if she's afraid to catch the ball!

Parent: I used to be afraid of getting hit by the baseball, too. I think it's pretty brave of Angie to play even though she's afraid sometimes. That takes a lot of courage.

Athlete: I still think she's a wuss.

Parent: I think maybe you're upset that you struck out every time you got up to bat today, and you're trying to make yourself feel better by ragging on Angie.

Athlete: I am not!

Parent: Okay, if you say so. You know, maybe you and Angie could get together for some extra practice time. You're not afraid of the ball at all—maybe you could teach her how to feel more comfortable when the ball comes to her.

Athlete: She could sure use the help, that's for sure.

Parent: And then she could help you with your batting.

Athlete: There's nothing wrong with my batting!

Parent: But even good batters can improve by practicing. And helping you would probably really boost Angie's confidence. That would be another way to help her become better at catching the ball. It would certainly be more helpful than calling her a wuss.

Athlete: Hmph. Well, maybe I could try it.

9. **Self-seeking.** Self-seeking isn't quite the same as show-boating, although people who showboat are definitely self-seeking. Athletes who continually seek after their own selfish interests are disrespectful because they're saying their wants and needs have more value than someone else's. Again, one of the dangers of sport

is that its competitive nature combined with all the adulation and attention we tend to shower on our sports superstars can lead athletes to become more selfish than they might otherwise be. A quarterback who ignores a wide-open receiver so that he can be the one to run the ball into the end zone is being selfish and disrespectful. A point guard (and I could give a lot of examples here!) who takes shot after shot instead of setting up plays for his or her teammates is being selfish and disrespectful. The younger your children are, the greater the tendency will be for them to fall into the self-seeking trap. You can encourage them to think of others more by complimenting them for every unselfish play they make.

10. **Celebrating.** When I talk about celebrating being disrespectful, I'm not referring to a spontaneous "high-five" after a good play or a score. I'm talking about the kind of celebrating that rubs the other team's nose in it. For example, in the same BYU-Hawaii game I mentioned earlier, a Hawaii wide receiver received two unsportsmanlike conduct penalties and was ejected from the game after he punted the ball into the stands and then leaped into the crowd to celebrate catching the touchdown pass that gave Hawaii fifty-two points (to BYU's twenty-four). Understandably, Hawaii was excited at so decisively beating the nation's ninth-ranked team. But acting the way this player did not only shows disrespect toward the competition, it also takes some of the luster off Hawaii's win.

One of the reasons the friend whose letter I shared earlier likes the Utah Jazz so much is that she feels the team reflects a "habit of respect" that is seldom seen in today's professional sports—or any sports arena, for that matter. Sportswriters familiar with the Jazz have noted that the idea of respect—for the game, for their coach, for the team—seems to be a core part of the team's philosophy. From their first team meeting, new Jazz players are taught what is expected of them. They are expected to have their shoes tied, their shirts tucked in, and to stay dressed after a game until the coach is finished speaking to them. After a game, win or lose, they are expected to exit the floor quickly. They are expected to be on time for practices and games. Jazz management feels that anything less is unprofessional, and shows a lack of respect for the job the players are paid to do.

We may not think of such little things as tucking in a shirt or tying a shoelace as being a big deal, but these little things add up and become part of other aspects of our lives—in other words, that "habit of respect" I talked about. As parents, it is often the "little things" we do for our children—picking them up on time from soccer practice, acting interested when their friends come running up to tell us about the big play they made, and so on—that help them develop a habit of respect in their own lives.

In contrast to the Jazz, there are other professional players who think nothing of showing up for practice late, or using the game as an excuse to show up other players. For example, in a basketball game that took place several years ago between the Orlando Magic and the Detroit Pistons, the Magic were up by twenty-one points with just over four seconds left in the game. Anthony Bowie was starting at forward for the injured Nick Anderson. Bowie was having a great game—twenty points, nine rebounds, and nine assists. Bowie got the rebound (giving him a double-double), but instead of letting the last four seconds run out called a time-out so he could set up a play that would allow him to get a triple-double. Pistons coach Doug Collins, outraged at Bowie's behavior, ordered his players not to defend. Bowie got his triple, but his selfishness cost him a loss of respect on the part of his opponents. And it didn't set a very good example for all of the young people who were watching.

Developing Respect in Your Children

The best way to develop respectful children is to treat them with respect. Parents, whether intentionally or not, don't always do a good job of this. We're stressed, we're busy, we think, "Hey, I'm the one who brought you into this world and gave you everything—you owe me!" So we take shortcuts. We forget "please" and "thank you" and resort to "Do it!" and "Because I said so!"

Since the athletes had their list, I think it's only fair that I provide a list of ten ways parents can show respect for their children.

Ten Ways Parents Can Show Respect for Their Children

1. **Listen to them.** Parents are so busy these days that much of the time we only listen to our kids with half an ear. Then we turn around and yell at them when they do the same thing to us! As much as possible, give your children your full attention. You'll be surprised at how good it makes them feel.

2. **Be open to learning from them.** When you are willing to learn from your kids, they are more willing to learn from you.

3. **Try to understand them.** There is a reason why Stephen Covey has sold millions of books. The reason is that the principles he teaches are timeless. My favorite is "seek first to understand, then to be understood." When we work to understand what someone else is thinking or feeling, it says to that person, "I'm putting your needs before mine. I value you. I think you're important." Understanding means recognizing that your child's feelings (unlike his or her actions) are neither right nor wrong. They just

are. If your child expresses a feeling you don't like ("I *hate* that stupid ref!") you can't say, "You don't really feel that way," because he or she *does* feel that way. You don't need to agree with your child's feelings, but you do need to validate them. Right: "Yes, I can see why fouling out of the game would make you feel really upset." Wrong: "What are you so upset about? You deserved every single one of those fouls!"

4. **Have dialogues, not monologues.** When you're the only one talking, all the attention is focused on you. That's okay if you're a stand-up comedian, but it's not very effective if you're a parent.

5. **Avoid probing, advising, and judging.** The point here is that children need to explore issues and make decisions without being pushed into them or unduly influenced by their parents. I'll illustrate this with an example. Let's say your child, who has been a starter all season, comes home and announces that he will not be starting in Friday night's game. Surprised, you say, "Oh, really? That must be upsetting." (Good—you're showing empathy.)

"Yeah, it sucks big-time," your verbally precocious offspring replies. You wait for details. None are forthcoming.

"So, uh, any idea why the coach put you on the bench?"

"Coach is an idiot."

It is at this point that you have to make a decision. Do you continue to ask questions to get to the bottom of what is going on (probing), or do you back off and let your child take the lead on what—and when—he is going to tell you? Of course, the fear is always there that if you don't ask questions, your children will never tell you anything. So it turns into kind of a delicate balancing act (as so much of parenting is). To demonstrate respect, what you want to do is act in a way that will encourage your children to open up to you and will also encourage them to discover answers to problems on their own. In the case of the benched athlete, I might go with one more question ("What makes you think the coach is an idiot?"), but if the answer is something to the effect of "because he just is, that's all!" then I would just drop it for a while. I would certainly not respond by saying: "You know, it's that kind of attitude that probably got you benched in the first place!" (judging) or, "Why don't you call your coach right now and see if you can meet with him to work this out?" (advising). In all likelihood, your patience will pay off and your child will unburden himself, knowing that he can do so freely and without pressure.

6. **Honor their dreams.** I know of one kid who, because of his size (six feet, two inches, 250 pounds), was pursued all through junior high and high school by people who wanted him to try out for the football team. But he didn't want to play football. He wanted to play tennis. I know that this young man's father, especially, would have loved to see his son out on the football field. But he didn't let on to that. So the boy played tennis quite happily (albeit not very well) and now looks back on his school sports experience with fond memories. But what if his dad had pushed him to play football, or let him know how disappointed he was in his son's decision to play tennis? What would his sports memories be like now? And how would his relationship with his dad be affected?

7. **Let your kids think for themselves.** Because we don't want to see our children get hurt, we sometimes try to make their decisions for them. Sometimes we just think we know better—what's the use of all our life experience, anyway, if not to pass it on to somebody? Well, you *can* pass that life experience on, but there's a respectful way and a disrespectful way. The disrespectful way is

to say, "I don't think you should play football, because I wasn't any bigger than you when I was in ninth grade and when I tried playing football, I got the snot beat out of me." The respectful way is to say, "You know, I was about your build when I was in ninth grade, and when I tried to play football it didn't turn out to be a very pleasant experience for me. My solution was to get into wrestling, where I was able to compete against people in my own weight category. I found that much more rewarding." Having said that, you shut your mouth. Then you proceed to number 8.

8. Support their choices. Whatever information or (solicited) advice you give your children should always be followed with "But whatever you decide, I will support your decision." (Assuming your child's decision doesn't involve doing something that will cause him or her serious physical or psychological harm.)

9. Be kind and considerate. We are usually kinder and more considerate to friends, neighbors, and coworkers than we are to members of our own family. That's because we know our family is pretty much stuck with us. And children are the most "stuck" of all, because they depend on us for their support. In other words, they are vulnerable. When kids show disrespect to their parents, they open themselves up to punishment: being grounded, having privileges revoked, etc. But when parents show disrespect to their kids, are the kids allowed to punish the parents? Not likely. Because parents are the ones in the position of power, it is even more important for them to act with kindness and consideration to their children. It will send a lifelong message of respect.

10. Seek their permission before acting on their behalf. Even if you follow suggestions 1 through 9 to the letter, there will be times when you may need to step in and act for your child. Maybe your child is having a problem with the coach that he or she hasn't been able to resolve on his or her own. Maybe you don't agree with the coach's philosophy on sportsmanship (even though your child doesn't have a problem with it). You need to ask permission from your child before you step in. Of course, the question then becomes, "What if my kid doesn't give me permission?" Then you need to use your judgment as to whether it's an issue you still need to act on. If your child's safety is at stake, then you must act. If not, then maybe there are other ways to work around the problem. For example, if you don't think the coach is teaching good sportsmanship but your son or daughter insists he or she will die a million deaths if you confront the coach about it, you need to think about other ways you can make up for the coach's shortcomings.

Respecting Opponents

One weekend while visiting my granddaughters and attending the traditional "Big Game" between Stanford and Cal, I was treated to a delightful display of sportsmanship. Stanford wide receiver Teyo Johnson was being interviewed about the game and, considering Cal's abysmal 0–9 record, could have disparaged the team considerably. Instead, Johnson talked about Cal's wonderful location, excellent academic reputation, and so on. He focused on the positive and quietly overlooked the rest. Johnson provided everyone with a perfect example of how to respect your opponent.

When the central focus of every practice session and every game is to beat the opponent, it becomes easy for athletes to see their competitors as "the enemy." When that happens, it is then easy for them to see respecting the opposition as a sign of weakness.

In actuality, the opposite is true. It takes a strong individual to step outside of himself or herself and say, "Wow, the other team played a great game today."

Stephen Covey offers this example of his son, Sean, who was a college quarterback. "When he was sacked, he'd hop back up, pat the tackler on the back, and say, 'Good hit.'"[4] What a great example of respect and sportsmanship!

Respect for opponents is not something that young athletes naturally develop. Rather, it is a quality that coaches and parents need to consciously work to instill.

How can you go about accomplishing this? In addition to the things we have talked about previously, you need to remind your children that their opponents provide them with opportunities to excel. Opponents give them the opportunity to stretch, to grow. They improve their skills more when there is someone competing against them than when they are trying to improve on their own.

Remind them, too, that human excellence is worthy of respect. For example, who could watch someone like Michael Jordan or Tiger Woods without being in absolute awe of the way they perform? Even the people playing against them come away impressed.

Encourage your children to always give their best effort, even when they know they're going to lose. Have you ever wondered how a player or a team that was behind by too many points to win could continue to play hard? The answer is simple: giving in shows a lack of respect for your competitor and yourself.

Help your children understand that when they make a spectacular play, it's usually because they've beaten a worthy opponent who has made their efforts look all the better. For instance, after the U.S. women's soccer team beat China to win the World Cup in 1999, members of the team showed their respect for their opponents by visiting the Chinese in their locker room. As backup goalkeeper Saskia Webber explained, "My mom is a person who always feels something for the others. She always makes a comment, 'You won, but they worked so hard, too.' I remembered how incredibly upset I was in 1995 [when the U.S. lost to Norway in the World Cup final]. That's why I wanted to go into the Chinese locker room. In '95, Norway did that little march in front of us and they walked away. There was no real respect there. For us to be able to communicate with the Chinese, even though they spoke little English, I thought was great. I wanted to go in there, to show them some respect."[5]

But what do you do if all your efforts to get your children to act respectfully toward their opponents are for naught, because of coaches who are making just as great an effort to get their players to see opponents as objects to be crushed? If you're lucky, you will have developed the kind of relationship with your kids that will allow them to weigh the values they learn at home against the ones they learn in sports and choose the better ones.

However, it is not uncommon for children to view authority figures outside their family (coaches, teachers, etc.) as the true authorities on life while the authority figures within their family (parents) are seen as well-meaning but misguided idiots. So when your child responds to your comments about "worthy opponents" by gleefully proclaiming, "Coach says we're gonna squash 'em like bugs!" don't get angry and don't turn it into a popularity contest between you and your child's coach.

Instead, calmly remind your child that in your family you try to speak of other people with respect. Say that while you respect the coach's right to his or her opinion, you don't necessarily agree with the way it was said. If you feel the coach's attitude is a major issue that you need to confront, get your child's buy-off on talking with the coach. In light of September 11, many coaches—along with people in general—have become more sensitive to being respectful of others, even when those others are on the opposite side. If you let the coach know that your goal isn't to make your child any less competitive, but to make your child a better competitor *and* a better person, then the coach will probably be more understanding of your efforts.

Respecting Officials

I grew up to always respect authority and respect those in charge.
                                    —Grant Hill, Detroit Pistons[6]

If you think it is challenging to teach your children to respect their opponents, it may be even more challenging to teach them to respect those individuals who oversee the game. For some reason, the notion has developed among many of today's athletes, coaches, and spectators that the sole job of officials is to rain on everybody's parade. I don't know why this is, but I suspect that the reason officials seem to be coming down harder on players these days is because so few of the players are giving them (and the rules) the respect they deserve.

Fortunately for officials, not everyone acts that way. Early in my basketball officiating career, I was working an inter-sectional game between the national champion UCLA Bruins and the perennial powerhouse Kansas Jayhawks. UCLA was full-court pressing as they always did in the Wooden years. Early in the game I called a ten-second violation on Kansas for their failure to get the ball over the half-court line inside of ten seconds—which I mistakenly thought was the amount of time they had to accomplish that. (Ask most people how much time a team has to cross midcourt and they will probably say, as I did, that you get ten seconds. But on an inbounds play at your end of the court moving up court you get five seconds to inbound the ball plus another ten to get it into the front court. So it is really fifteen seconds altogether.) As I remember it, I made that mistake several times during the contest. The Kansas coach could have gone berserk, assuming that he understood the technicality (and I believe he did), but he remained calm and controlled and gentlemanly throughout the contest. After the game he reviewed the films and confirmed that I was starting my ten-second count too early. Nevertheless, throughout the game he showed nothing but respect for my position as an official.

No system can exist without a set of rules and regulations. Without officials, sports would not exist. Officials represent the integrity of the game. People who harass officials are subjecting them to psychological abuse. In effect, they're saying that the official is stupid, inept, biased, or just plain cheating. However, the fact that there are supervisors at every game who evaluate the officials makes it highly unlikely that any of these assertions are true.

Victor Matheson, a USSF National Referee with fifteen years' experience, relates the story of an incident that occurred at an Under-10 tournament he once worked. One coach became so verbally abusive of a teenage referee after she made a bad call that the ref was finally forced to abandon the match, leaving the two teams without a game. What call did the ref miss? She allowed an illegal substitution. Matheson makes the point that, yes, the duty of the referee is to know the rules, but it was a minor infraction that in all probability would have had no effect on the outcome of the game. It certainly wasn't worth the coach getting so agitated over.

As Matheson reminds us, the motto of U.S. Youth Soccer is "the game for kids." This motto could apply to any youth sports organization. Thus, anything coaches, fans, or referees do to distract kids from their game is disrespectful of them.

Remember what our original definition of respect was? Respect means recognizing that a person, situation, or thing has value. Recognizing an individual's value means viewing that person within a whole context. An official needs to be seen as a person with feelings, dreams, and goals. Officials need to be seen as human beings who sometimes make mistakes. They have families that care about them. They have problems and worries of their own. In other words, officials are not just objects in the athlete's path to glory.

Parents need to help their children recognize that being a game official is a thankless (literally—how many times have you ever thanked the ref after a game?) job that most officials fill not because they're into power or control or have a secret desire to make people's lives miserable. Rather, they do it because they love the game. Instead of remembering the occasional bad call, we need to admire and respect the person with the courage to take the game into his or her own hands to see that it is played right.

How can you help your children to see this? If they're old enough, you might encourage them to try officiating, themselves. Most youth sports leagues are in desperate need of people to oversee games, and would welcome your child's involvement.

Another project you could try is to have your children pick out an official (either one they see on television or someone from their own sports league) and find out more about that person. What kind of sports background does the person have? How long has he or she been an official? How did the official get started? Why did he or she want to become an official? What are the best and worst parts about the official's job?

The object of doing these things is to get your kids to see beyond the uniform to the person who is wearing it. Once you can get them to do that, you will have gone a long way toward helping them develop the empathy and understanding that is such an integral part of respecting others.

Respecting Teammates

A couple times a week I play a pickup game of basketball with guys who range in age from their twenties to their fifties. About the only thing we have in common is we all love the game. Some of the players are pretty good. Others aren't very good but want to learn. Still others aren't very good and have no interest in learning. I really think some of these guys believe the main purpose of basketball is to get as many shots as you can. Consequently, they shoot every time they get their hands on the ball. This frustrates me to no end! Sometimes I have to literally bite my tongue to keep from saying something. Then there are times when I'm sure my body language says it all.

I guess the lesson I've learned here is that no matter how old you are, it can still be a challenge to respect your teammates!

You would think that respect of one's teammates (and, by extension, one's coach—since coaches and players are all on the same team) would be a natural part of sports. But one only needs to read the sports pages to find countless examples of players being disrespectful of their teammates and coaches, and coaches being disrespectful of their players. One of the most famous examples of this is the Latrell Sprewell situation, when the Golden State Warrior player became so incensed at Coach P. J. Carlesimo's verbal abuse that he put a stranglehold on Carlesimo's throat.

On a smaller scale, there's the case of the adolescent player who argued that other less-skilled teammates shouldn't get the chance to play in important games because they weren't good enough. The boy's rationale was that his father didn't become wealthy by choosing less-talented people over more-talented people when a critical business decision was on the line. The fallacy with this argument is that sport is not the same as business. The object of business is to make money. The object of sport (youth sports, anyway) is to allow young people to have fun and develop skills— including the skill of learning how to stay cool in pressure situations. They can't do that if they don't get to play in important games.

I can clearly remember one time when I unwittingly showed disrespect toward my teammates and coach. It was during my senior year in high school. Our basketball team, which would eventually go undefeated, was playing in a preseason tournament.

Hampered by having two of our starters out with the flu, we nevertheless made it to the finals, where we were playing our league rival—Long Beach Wilson.

The clock was ticking down, the score was tied, and I took the last shot of the game. As the ball clanked off the rim, Long Beach called a time-out. Unfortunately, they had no more time-outs left. They were whistled for the technical.

My teammates and I huddled around our coach to plan our strategy. I was chosen to shoot the technical. If I made it, the game and the tournament would be ours.

It was at that point that I nobly announced to our coach, "Hey, I'm going to miss the free throw on purpose and we are going to beat them fair-and-square in overtime." You see, a lot of the Wilson players were my friends from our basketball days at the Long Beach YMCA, and I thought that by sending the game into overtime I'd be doing the right thing by them. In the insensitivity of youth, I didn't think about whether I was doing the right thing by my coach and teammates who had worked so hard to win.

The coach just grabbed me by the wrist, squeezed very hard, and said, "You miss this shot and you won't play another minute the rest of the season."

Well, I made the free throw and we won the game and went 32–0 for the season, and I ended up being voted player of the year for California. Even more, I learned a lesson about respect that has stuck with me to this day.

When you respect others, you treat them the way you want to be treated. Forgive me for using another Stanford story, but this one tickles me. Locker rooms are not usually known for their polite language, but when Mark "Mad Dog" Madsen (currently with the Los Angeles Lakers) played basketball for Stanford the locker room talk went from an "R" rating to "PG." That's because Madsen is an active member of The Church of Jesus Christ of Latter-Day Saints (Mormon) who served a two-year mission for his church. "It's not like I'd be offended or get mad," Madsen said at the time, "but I appreciate the effort the guys make. It's not something I've asked them to do. It's just something they do."

Now of course, it wasn't Madsen's religion that had his team-mates toning down their language—it was the example that he set. Madsen was known as a good leader and a no-ego kind of guy who got just as much of a thrill out of seeing his teammates do well as he did his own successes. He set an example for his team-mates of leadership and respect, and they respected him back.

Respecting your teammates means giving credit to their skills and performances. It means assuming they are trying to do the best they can. Respecting others means accepting them and their actions—even when they make a mistake or have a subpar per-formance. You may not be happy, but that's where being a good sport comes in—the way you react when a teammate or a coach blows it.

How do you get this message across to your kids in a way they'll understand and appreciate (especially if they've just expe-rienced losing a game because a teammate fumbled the ball or called a nonexistent time-out)? As always, the prime teacher is the example you set. For instance, do you come home from work ranting and raving about the account you would have landed if only "Bailey hadn't blown it by dropping the ball on those adver-tising figures"?

Another effective teaching method is to use stories (which is why I've tried to include a lot of them in this book). Here's a story you could share with your kids that illustrates the importance of using positive reinforcement with their teammates:

Dot Richardson remembers warming up with a teammate of hers soon after she'd signed on with the women's professional softball team as a thirteen-year-old. "I made a bad throw, so I said, 'Oh!

Sorry, Mary Lou!' And Mary Lou said to me, 'Don't ever say sorry to me again, because I know you didn't mean to throw it like that. I know you're doing your best.' "[7]

One thing I think you need to point out to your children is that respect doesn't mean you have to like the other person. As a former minister, I believe firmly in the need to try to love everyone. But I also understand that this is a really hard thing to do. Even if you don't like someone on your team, that doesn't mean you need to treat the person meanly or say unkind things to him or her.

Respect also means that when you do like a person, it shouldn't be because he or she is the best player on the team. Respect is showing your teammates that they are valued for who they are, not for how many home runs they get or how many tackles they make. (Here's another one of those illustrative stories.) Three walk-on members of the University of Southern California's basketball team finally walked *off* the team after one too many incidents of being made to feel like their contributions weren't valued. It didn't matter that they sometimes weren't allowed to share the postgame pizza given to the scholarship athletes, or given the warm-up suits and shoes the other team members got. But when a team manager told them they couldn't sit on the bench at games anymore, they asked Coach Henry Bibby for an explanation. His alleged response: "[Bleep] that, you guys either suit up and sit behind the bench or you guys are off the team for good! I don't need to talk to anybody that's a walk-on on this team."[8]

The increased focus on winning, along with the importance of securing a college scholarship, can lead to a cutthroat environment where players can see their own teammates as obstacles in their path to success. In addition, the increasing number of females who are playing with and against males in contact sports such as wrestling and football is bringing challenges for players, coaches, and parents. Players have refused to play against (or with) them. Boys wonder if it is more respectful to "go easy" on female players. Girls are harassed by opponents and teammates alike. What parents must remember is that there is no place for this kind of behavior in good sports, and parents should encourage their athletic children to treat *all* of their teammates with respect and consideration.

To me, respect is a mosaic—with athletes providing the color and flair, coaches the guidance and structure, parents and fans the support, and the officials the structure to maintain the beauty and integrity of the game. Without everyone's contributions, we cannot have good sports. Thus, everyone is to be valued and respected for what he or she brings to the game.

MODEL–TEACH–ENCOURAGE

1. Discuss the "Top Ten Ways Parents Can Teach Respect" with your children. Ask them how they would grade you in the different areas. Ask for suggestions on how you can do better.
2. Discuss the "Top Ten Ways Athletes Show Disrespect." Ask your children if they can recognize any of their own actions in these illustrations.
3. Improve your listening skills by reading a book or article on reflective listening. Try to implement what you learn with your children.
4. Work at seeing sports from your children's perspective. Ask them to name some of their best sports memories. Ask them what their sports goals are. Learn their top five reasons for playing sports.

5. Do not allow your children to use name-calling or rude talk when referring to other people. Have open conversations with your children and within your family regarding appropriate ways to communicate with others.
6. Respect your children's choices. If your highly skilled child prefers to play on a team with his or her friends versus an elite team where he or she doesn't know anyone, then you need to respect that decision.
7. Avoid, if possible, disciplining or rebuking your children in front of their peers. This can result in a child feeling that he or she needs to show off by becoming more disrespectful.
8. Speak respectfully to your children. Refrain from making unkind or negative comments. This can be hard sometimes, when faced with the pressures and disappointments of sports. But your children should never hear you say anything hurtful about their efforts.
9. Treat other sports participants with respect. Do not let your children hear you say bad things about their coach, the officials, other athletes, etc. If there is a problem, go directly to the person and talk with him or her.
10. Remember that your children have the right to play without being embarrassed by your comments. If you absolutely, positively cannot make it through a game without spouting off, then be sure to sit far enough away that your comments can't be heard by others. Better yet, go sit in your car.
11. Respect the coach's knowledge, decisions, and rules. Make the effort to learn more about the game so that you better understand the complexity of the decisions the coach sometimes has to make. Allow coaches to guide your children without butting in.

12. Don't tell the coach what to do. ("Put my kid in!") Instead, ask the coach what your children can do better to achieve their goals.

13. Make the effort to thank the coaches. Teach your children to say thank you, too. This is part of teaching your children to recognize and appreciate what other people do for them.

14. Recognize the officials' role and the benefit they bring to the game. Do not publicly question an official's judgment and never his or her honesty.

15. Make a habit of greeting the other athletes on your children's teams, or of congratulating them after the game. Do the same with opponents. Know everyone's name. Try to learn opponents' names, if possible. Do things that help show your children that you see these people as individuals.

16. Applaud good plays by your team and by members of the opposing team. Cheer for your children and their teams to play well. Don't cheer against the opponent.

17. At the end of a sporting event, shake hands with the parents of the opposing team. This shows the athletes that their parents know how to be good sports.

18. Children who watch sports on television will often see examples of athletes, coaches, and others acting disrespectfully toward officials or one another. Take advantage of these moments to discuss what is happening with your children. Ask them how they think the person who is being disrespected feels. Ask them what would be a better way to handle the situation.

19. Pay close attention to the messages your children are getting from television, movies, toys, games, music, and literature. Many of today's television shows and movies feature children who act disrespectfully toward others.

When the messages your children are getting conflict with the values you are trying to teach, speak up. Make it clear how you would expect them to behave in a similar situation.

20. Help your children understand the difference between disagreeing with someone and being threatening or confrontational. Teach them how to disagree respectfully.

A Good Sport Cooperates with Others

Unfortunately, our heroes are not the guys who say, "Let's see if we can sit down and work this out."
—CAROL TAVRIS, SOCIAL PSYCHOLOGIST AND AUTHOR OF
ANGER: THE MISUNDERSTOOD EMOTION[1]

What does the ability to cooperate with others have to do with sportsmanship? You might think not very much. Sport is generally thought of as a win/lose proposition—people are competing, or working against each other, with the final outcome being one winner and one loser. Cooperation, on the other hand, is characterized as people working together to come up with a mutually agreeable solution. Cooperating is about being unselfish, about thinking of others. It's about being willing to meet people halfway. It's about being able to see another person's perspective.

Cooperation naturally follows respect. When we respect others, we are more likely to cooperate with them. And when we cooperate with others, we are showing that we respect their feelings, their needs, and their points of view.

But sport is a competitive arena. It is highly unlikely that we would ever turn on "Monday Night Football" to find the announcers saying, "The official has just tossed the coin and the captains have elected to play to a 21–21 tie." However, within the sports arena are many opportunities for individuals to cooperate with one another.

The one that most obviously comes to mind, of course, is cooperating with one's teammates in order to win. But that is not the only opportunity athletes have for cooperation. Athletes also have opportunities to cooperate, or work together, with the officials, their opponents, even the spectators in the stands, to ensure a more positive and uplifting sports experience for everyone.

One reason why sport is not generally seen as a training ground for cooperative behavior relates to our Western culture. When the United States was first settled, men were trained to respond to challenges or threats with aggression. In order to be prepared to defend their property, males were taught to be alert to the least slight to their masculinity. While the need for this kind of "super-macho" behavior no longer exists, the behavior itself often does. What's more, it is no longer the exclusive province of males. As women have entered the business world and the sports world in greater numbers, many have felt that in order to compete, they need to match their behavior to that of their male counterparts.

Another thing that makes it challenging to instill cooperation in sport is that ours is a culture of confrontation. Deborah Tannen calls it "the argument culture" (in her 1999 book, *The Argument Culture*). Rather than working things out, we take pride in being stubborn and "sticking to our guns." In our nation's capital, this way of not doing business has even been given a name. They call it *gridlock*. Basically, no one is willing to move or give way, so everyone ends up suffering the consequences.

Understanding this background may help you to be more patient if your attempts to encourage cooperative behavior in your athletic children (especially boys) are met with resistance. However, just as our country benefited from the inspiring display of cooperation demonstrated by lawmakers after the events of September 11, so, too, can sports benefit from the cooperation shown by athletes toward their fellow sports participants.

Defining Cooperation

Competition and cooperation are not opposites. I see competition as (ideally) a form of cooperation, a framework for doing one's best in concert with other people who are simultaneously doing their best, thus inspiring you to do even better.
—Mariah Burton Nelson, *Embracing Victory:*
Life Lessons in Competition and Compassion[2]

One reason people believe cooperation doesn't play a big role in sports is that they think cooperation means an absence of conflict—and in sports, conflict is part of the nature of the game. But cooperation doesn't mean not having any conflict. After all, conflict is part of growth. Children who never experience conflict—whose parents smooth out all life's little bumps and bruises for them—are in for a world of hurt when they grow up.

What cooperation really involves is knowing how to reduce conflict and minimize its disruptive influence. It means you can have disagreements in a hockey game without resorting to a bench-clearing brawl. It means if you're a professional baseball player and a fan swipes your cap, you and your teammates don't need to jump into the stands to forcibly retrieve it. You are able to resolve conflict in an effective, constructive manner—one that leaves everyone whole, in the broadest sense of the term.

Cooperation is also defined as any activity that involves the willing interdependence of two or more individuals. When it comes to raising children, adults often confuse this kind of coop-eration with compliance. Compliance is simply obedience to rules or authority. It is not intentional cooperation.

To see the difference between compliance and cooperation, all I have to do is tell my grandson, Christian, that he "must" share his favorite toy with his little brother, Cayleb. Under these cir-cumstances, Christian's compliance usually takes the form of throwing the toy at his brother and then storming out of the room in tears.

On the other hand, if I sit down with Christian and explain that "Papa" (his name for me) has some important work to get done and I need his help in entertaining Cayleb until I finish and does he have any suggestions for how we could do this, Christian will often be the one to suggest playing with the beloved toy, and will cheerfully take the initiative in giving it to Cayleb. This is true cooperation.

As you have probably experienced with your own children, negative methods (yelling, nagging, demanding) of trying to enlist their cooperation don't usually work. Children who com-ply only because they're being yelled at or threatened are doing so out of fear, not out of a desire to show cooperative, responsi-ble behavior.

It is also important for parents to realize that what we adults see as uncooperative behavior is often our child's struggle to develop independence. Because we do want our children to become independent, we need to find ways that allow them to feel powerful and valuable that don't come at the expense of others. For example, with Christian, I asked him for his ideas on how we could entertain his brother. Being consulted in this way made him feel important and "in charge."

In his book *The 7 Habits of Highly Effective People*, Stephen Covey discusses the issue of cooperation at length when he talks about going for the "win/win."

Win/win means that agreements or solutions are mutually beneficial, mutually satisfying. With a win/win solution, all parties feel good about the decision and feel committed to the action plan. Win/win sees life as a cooperative, not a competitive arena. Most people tend to think in terms of dichotomies: strong or weak, hardball or softball, win or lose. But that kind of thinking is fundamentally flawed. It's based on power and position rather than on principle. Win/win is based on the paradigm that there is plenty for everybody, that one person's success is not achieved at the expense or exclusion of the success of others.[3]

Now, of course, in athletic competition, one person's or one team's success usually *is* achieved at the expense or exclusion of the success of others—*if success is defined solely in terms of winning.* However, if you and your children define success as putting forth one's best effort and enjoying and learning from the experience, then you see that it is possible for everyone to walk away from sports with a win/win.

Mariah Burton Nelson, a former professional basketball player who writes frequently on the subject of sports, defines competition as "seeking excellence together." She points out that the word *compete* comes from the Latin *competere*, which means "to seek together."[4]

As you strive to instill this spirit of "cooperative competition" in your children, you need to ask yourself, "What example am I setting? How do I usually interact with people? Do I have a win/lose mentality, or a win/win? When my children and I have disagreements, is it more important to me that I 'win,' or that we come away feeling like we both got what we wanted?" Child-rearing expert Elizabeth Pantley advises, "Getting to win-win takes negotiation. Parents can assist their children by responding to a child's demands, 'That sounds like a good way for you to win. And I want you to win. But I want to win, too. Can you think of a solution that works for both of us?'"[5]

Cooperating with Teammates

I remember reading about a baseball coach who gave each of his players a T-shirt with a picture on it of a bunch of guys clinging to a rope and the slogan "24 Guys Hanging on the Same Rope." Over two hundred years ago Benjamin Franklin pronounced the same sentiments when he informed the nation's founders that they must all hang together, or assuredly they'd all hang separately.

Teamwork has been around for a long time. Today it's more popular than ever. How popular? Amazon.com shows more than two hundred business books with the word *team* in the title.

What is it about teamwork that gives the concept such staying power? Teams make a real difference. That's because teams have synergy—meaning when people work together to achieve a common goal, the result is often far greater than the sum of its parts.

At the 1980 Winter Olympics in Lake Placid, New York, we saw an amazing demonstration of this kind of synergy. At the time, with the Cold War still raging, there was nothing like a victory over the Soviet Union to stir American pride. However, few people entertained the notion that the American hockey team could pull off such a victory.

The American team, with an average age of twenty-two, had no superstars. Instead, Coach Herb Brooks used a special psychological test to select ten unselfish team players who were adaptable, responded well to pressure, and would support one another. These players were willing to set their egos aside and channel their efforts toward a shared goal.

They were heavy underdogs. In fact, just before the Olympic games, the Russians had blown the Americans off the ice by a score of 10–3 in Madison Square Garden.

But when the rematch came in the showdown for the Olympic gold medal, the United States was ready. The final score was United States four, U.S.S.R. three. When the final horn blew, pandemonium filled the arena, as hockey sticks and American flags waved proudly.

As individuals, the Americans had been good. But as a team, they were transformed into an unbeatable skating machine. They took one plus one and made it equal three.

Cooperating with teammates means working together—like the U.S. hockey team did—to achieve a goal. It means focusing on interdependence versus independence. Simply put, it is a "we" and "our" attitude versus a "me" and "mine" attitude.

Young athletes are often so wrapped up in their own performances and challenges that they don't look outside themselves to see how they could be working with their teammates to help them (and the team) be better. One mom I know faced this challenge on her very first foray into youth sports. The problem wasn't with her own son, but with one of his teammates. The boy (whose dad happened to be a coach) was head-and-shoulders better than any of the other players on the team. Consequently, instead of taking practice drills seriously, he would goof off. He'd pass the ball over his shoulder, or through his legs—making it difficult for teammates to catch it, and seriously distracting the other boys from their learning efforts.

Since the team parents had been encouraged to help with practices as much as they wanted, the mom solved the problem (temporarily, at least) by standing beside the boy and saying, "You know, Aaron, you are so good at this stuff! I can see you've played a lot. Can you show the other boys the right way to do it so they can learn to be as good as you?"

Cooperating with teammates means filling your role well, whether it's that of first-stringer or bench warmer. When I look back on my high school basketball team that went 32–0, the thing I remember most is how well everyone played his role. It was the same for the team I was on my senior year at Stanford. Several key players had graduated; consequently, we weren't expected to do much that year. We ended up going 18–6 (with four of the losses by a point or two). For several decades, that record was the best in Stanford history—and it's all because each player knew his role and played it unselfishly.

Perhaps no one played his role better on that Stanford team than Ron Wagner. Ron's brother, Harold ("Hap"), was one of our starters. Ron had played a lot himself as a sophomore, but since then rarely got off the bench. Nevertheless, he was our best cheerleader. He never complained about his playing time, but instead was always positive and supportive, constantly observing play from where he sat and throwing out constructive suggestions.

Cooperating with teammates means making an effort to get along with everyone, even teammates who are difficult or unlikable. This is very, very hard for children to do without guidance and assistance from their parents, because it involves social skills that even many adults are lacking.

Tips for Helping Your Children Get Along with Difficult Teammates

1. Point out to your child that it's not the person he or she dislikes—it's that person's behavior.

2. Help your child identify the behavior that is bothering him or her. For example, is a teammate bossy? Is he or she always showing off, or acting like a know-it-all? Is the teammate too clingy—always following your child around and wanting to do everything your child does?

3. Have your child rate on a scale of one to ten how much the behavior bothers him or her. If it's less than five, maybe your child will decide it's just something he or she will put up with. If it's five

or greater, your child will probably feel better about taking action to change the behavior.

4. Help your child determine which course of action might work best: talking to the person about the behavior, or changing how he or she reacts to that person's behavior.

5. If your child decides to change how he or she reacts to the other person's behavior, help your child figure out what the best reaction might be. For instance, when a teammate is a know-it-all, your child might decide to think, "Yes, this person is annoying, but he is very knowledgeable, so I'm going to ignore his attitude and turn our relationship into a positive by trying to learn as much as I can from him."

6. If your child decides he or she wants to talk to the other person about the behavior, role-play the conversation with your child so he or she knows what to say. Here is an example:

Child:	Teresa, could I talk to you for a minute?
You (pretending to be Teresa):	Sure. What about?
Child:	It seems like just about every time I miss a shot or make a mistake, you make fun of me. It embarrasses me and makes me angry when you do that.
You (as Teresa):	Don't be so sensitive! I'm just teasing you!
Child:	Yes, but if you've ever been teased before, you know that sometimes teasing really hurts. The main point is, how you act when I screw up isn't helping me to play better. Don't you think we'd be a stronger team if everyone was able to play her best?

You (as Teresa):   Duh.

Child: Is there something you can think of that you
                    could say to me when I mess up that would
                    help me get it right the next time?

You (as Teresa):   How about if I just told you what you're
                    doing wrong?

Child: Okay. If you promise to let me know what
                    I'm doing wrong without teasing me about
                    it, then I promise not to get upset by the crit-
                    icism.

7. Explain to your child that often people act disagreeably
because they are trying to get attention (remind your child of
times he or she has done this). Encourage him or her to try giving disagreeable or unpleasant teammates more attention when
they are displaying positive behavior (for example, thank them for
encouraging you when you make a mistake). Hopefully, this will
help cut back on their negative behaviors.

Cooperating with teammates also requires that your children
understand that their behaviors and actions have a ripple effect.
They need to understand that they can either choose to pull their
team and their sport down by selfish, me-first behavior, or they
can choose to lift it up by setting an example of cooperation and
caring.

Often young athletes think that as long as their individual skills
are good, that's all that really matters. As a parent, you can remind
your children that most coaches prefer to have a roster full of team
players versus one or two "stars." When you have team players,
the "stars" may end up scoring less, but the team ends up scoring
a lot more. A coach needs to worry about maximizing the contributions of everyone, not just a few.

In addition, concentrating on teamwork helps build teams for the long haul. When athletes work to develop teammates' skills as well as their own, it really pays off the following season. That's why teamwork is so valued by coaches.

Cooperating with the Coach

Jackson, 54, ended his one-year sabbatical from the league last June. He left his rustic Montana cabin, moved into a beachfront Playa del Ray home and coaxed the three Lakers starters—O'Neal, Bryant and sharpshooter Glen Rice—who underachieved and overfussed their way to a postseason flameout last season to harmoniously work together on the same set.

—"Coaching Icon Poised for Another Title Run,"

USA Today, April 21, 2000[6]

LaVell Edwards, the BYU football coach who coached some of the country's top quarterbacks (Steve Young, Jim McMahon, and others), once said that of all the quarterbacks he had worked with, the one he admired most was Sean Covey. Covey was in line to be the Cougars' starting quarterback, but was benched in favor of a young upstart named Ty Detmer (who went on to win the Heisman Trophy). As Edwards explained, Covey didn't like it, but he didn't complain and he didn't whine. Instead, he did his best to be prepared in case the team should need him.

For athletes, cooperating with the coach means doing what the coach asks without arguing. It means following team rules. It means showing up on time for practices and games. It means being prepared. It means discussing concerns and problems with the coach, instead of complaining behind his or her back. Parents should always encourage and support this kind of cooperation in their children.

This cooperation is a two-way street. When I was coaching, I always understood that the key to success was creating an environment in which my athletes could develop to their fullest potential. Coaches who don't care can create an environment that will turn off the players—make them hate to go to practice, expend little effort, look for shortcuts, and pray for the whole experience to end quickly.

Since many parents also end up being coaches, I would like to talk about how coaches can maximize their team's talents without sapping their desire and enthusiasm. In other words, how do coaches build cooperative and cohesive teams?

I believe that the more democratic approach (viewing athletes as resources and partners) produces more successful and satisfied athletes. Coaches do this by:

- Involving players in decision making. Coaches should get their players' input into rules, practice times, etc. Where there is no involvement, there is also no commitment. When coaches encourage players to express their opinions and preferences, they will often find that the players come up with higher standards and stricter rules than the coach might have suggested.
- Targeting a common mission. Discuss season goals, where you want to be at the end of the season and the goals it will take to get there. This brings people together, gets them on the same page, and creates enthusiasm and belief in something meaningful.
- Discussing the specific goals it will take to reach your common mission.
- Communicating openly and often.
- Continually monitoring progress. How are we doing? Where do we need to improve? How can we get better?

- Establishing and rewarding roles. Not everyone can be a star. Every team needs people who will do the little things that often don't get the headlines but are essential to success.
- Daring to care. Leadership is about caring for players as individuals, not just athletes.

Coaches who exemplify this kind of cooperative behavior will find that they are building the spirit of cooperation in their athletes. In turn, athletes are more likely to extend that cooperation to others.

What should you do if you feel your child's coach isn't exactly a model of cooperative behavior? For instance, what if your child has a coach who tells the players, "I want us to work together as a team," but then pits one athlete against another? One option, of course, is to present the coach with a copy of this book with this section highlighted.

Another option would be to secure your child's permission to talk with the coach. You could approach the coach in a neutral way, by saying something like, "I'm trying to help Johnny improve his teamwork skills, because I know how much this would benefit the entire team. I don't think you realize some of the things you are doing are giving Johnny mixed messages about teamwork. For example (give some specific examples). . . . Is there a way that you could still accomplish your goal (of motivating the athletes or whatever) while helping the kids to understand the importance of teamwork?"

Cooperating with Officials

He's an all-star player with a right to voice his opinion. He's not going to change the way he speaks; that's who he is. They have to

*accept who he is. The officials can be a little quick with him. Some-
times it's the way Rasheed talks more than what he says.*
—Scottie Pippen, explaining why teammate Rasheed Wallace
received more than twice as many technical fouls as any
other NBA player during the 1999–2000 season[7]

Of all the poor excuses for not cooperating with others, "That's
just the way I am" is probably the worst. We hear different ver-
sions of this all the time. "Love me or leave me." "I'm too old to
change." "You can't teach an old dog new tricks." Again, what it
boils down to is lack of respect for others, or just plain laziness.
Cooperative behavior requires more effort than selfish behavior,
and some people just don't want to put forth that effort.

Does this mean that athletes have to accept every call an official makes with a smile on their face? No, it doesn't. It means that
when an athlete has a disagreement or concern (such as an opponent who is getting away with a lot of fouls), the athlete should
calmly discuss this with the referee. It does *not* mean the athlete
follows the official all the way down the sideline haranguing him
or her. Cooperating with officials means allowing them to do their
job so that everyone else can do theirs.

How can parents teach this kind of cooperation? First, you
should set the example yourself. Control your temper when calls
go against your children or their teams. Make sure you are familiar with the rules of the game so that you understand the calls the
officials make. If your child complains about a bad call, feel free
to say, "You know, I didn't understand that one, either. Let's ask
your coach or look it up in the rule book to see if we can find out
why the official made that call."

Second, you should be clear about the kind of behavior you
expect from your children. ("I expect you to be an example to others of how to cooperate with the officials.")

Third, be specific about what constitutes cooperative behavior. ("I don't want to see you yelling, getting in the official's face, or following the official down the court.")

Finally, always remember to compliment your children when you see them modeling cooperative behavior. Remind them that you understand how hard it is to do it sometimes, but it is a skill that will serve them well for the rest of their lives.

Cooperating with Opponents

Jerry Fenton, a high school coach from Valley Center, California, shared a great story with me of one young athlete's spirit of cooperation:

> My team was an upstart team, going against the CIF power-house—a team that had not lost a league contest in five years. Meanwhile, my team was undefeated (3–0) with a history of three wins in the past three years. On my team I had a young girl who was an exceptional front runner. During the competition, the course made a "Y" at the mile mark, and my front runner started going the wrong way. Her closest competitor was about 80 yards behind. I was too far away to be heard. However, the girl who was in second place yelled loudly, *"You're going the wrong way!"* My athlete veered onto the correct course. If that girl had remained silent she could have won the race and her team won the event. I wish I could coach that quality of character into all my athletes.

Here is another one of my favorite stories of one athlete reaching out to another in the spirit of cooperation and competition:

> In the two-man bobsled trials at the 1964 Olympic Games in Innsbruck, Austria, Eugenio Monti and his partner, the Italian cham-

pions, had made a successful final run. They were in first place and only Tony Nash and his partner representing England were left to go. However, Nash had a broken part on his sled and could not do the final run.

Monti would be the winner but he felt badly for Nash. He considered removing the part from his own sled and giving it to Nash so he could compete.

Monti gave Nash the required part from his own sled. Nash made the repair, raced down the course in record time, and won. Monti had decided that everyone should have a fair chance of winning the competition. Four years later at the Olympic Winter Games in Grenoble, France, Eugenio Monti won the gold medal in the four-man bobsled event.[8]

Cooperating with opponents doesn't mean playing "down" so that the competition looks good or has a chance to win. It means playing the game in a way that both competitors have the opportunity to play their best.

This is more than just playing by the rules. Did the rules state that the second-place runner had to warn the first-place runner of her error? Did the rules state that Eugenio Monti had to give one of his sled parts to his competitor? No. The second-place runner could have kept her mouth shut. Eugenio Monti could have kept his sled part. They both would have been playing by the rules of the game, and they both would have won their races. But they wouldn't have been playing by the rules of good sportsmanship.

Cooperating with an opponent also means not escalating conflicts. When tennis player Lleyton Hewitt made remarks that implied an African American linesman at the 2001 U.S. Open was favoring Hewitt's African American opponent, the media jumped all over it. The opponent in the match, James Blake, could have made a big ruckus over Hewitt's comments (and gotten a ton of publicity in the process), but instead, he refused to be drawn into the conflict. You can encourage your children to follow the same example of graciousness. For example, if your child is being verbally assaulted by a trash-talking opponent, he or she can say, "Hey, I don't appreciate that kind of talk. Why don't we just play the game?" What your child *doesn't* need to do is respond in kind. Again, the point is to take whatever action will enable both sides to play their best. If your children can keep that objective in their minds when interacting with opponents, they will be following the actions of a good sport.

Cooperating and Problem Solving

Have you noticed that cooperating with other people often means being able to solve problems that you are having with them? That is why one of the most helpful skills you can teach your children is how to be effective problem solvers. You can begin by setting the example in the way you solve problems you are having with your children. You do this by:

- Choosing a quiet, uninterrupted time to address the problem.
- Defining the problem in unemotional terms.
- Letting your child give his or her side of the story, and listening quietly.
- Discussing as many possible solutions as you can come up with together.
- Jointly deciding which solution you will use, and then following through.

Remember that the key to having a successful problem-solving session is to *work together* with your child to arrive at a solution. If you have one solution in mind, and nothing else will satisfy you, then you really aren't open to problem solving at the moment.

You also help your children learn how to solve problems when you model flexibility and compromise. This means allowing your children to use valid reasons to get you to change a decision. I know of one dad who, stressed by work responsibilities, immediately forbade his son to attend a weekend practice when the boy didn't clean his room as he was asked to do. The son responded by saying, "That's not fair! You didn't warn me!" You see, in this particular family, it was a rule that children would receive one warning before a major punishment was handed down. The dad, though still angry and upset, was able to say, "You're right. I shouldn't have used your practice as a punishment. But I still think you need to have some kind of punishment. What do you think would be fair?" In this way, he was able to effectively model cooperation and problem solving for his son.

The Need for Cooperation—in Sports and Beyond

The events of September 11 brought home several truths to the American people. One of these truths is that there has never been a greater need for people to get along with one another.

September 11 also brought out a spirit of cooperation among people probably unequaled in its depth and scope. Americans, who for forty years had been progressively moving from "we" to "me" oriented, suddenly experienced a 360-degree turnaround.

As Amitai Etzioni, a sociology professor at George Washington University, suggested in a *USA Today* article, it would be helpful if we could continue to approach more matters not as confrontations between individual rights and the common good but as quests for finding ways to work things out. This is what he calls looking for the "golden middle."

The idea that one should look for the golden middle is a very ancient one, but that makes it no less valid. Neither individual rights nor the common good should be treated as absolutes. We should be looking for ways to serve both as much as possible. When no such ways can be found, we should hammer out a compromise.[9]

Whether we're talking about matters of homeland security or a neighborhood softball game, learning to live and work with others is necessary for success in life. Children who demonstrate a number of cooperative strategies and can attend to the needs of others while also asserting and defending their own rights are more likely to be socially successful and to establish mutually satisfying friendships.

On the other hand, aggressive or noncooperative behavior is a deterrent to friendships and social success. (Aggression should not be confused with assertion. Assertive behavior is when a person maintains and defends his or her own rights and concerns. Aggressive behavior is when one person tries to forcibly impose his or her wishes on someone else.)

As Stephen Covey says, "Interdependence is a higher value than independence."[10] Increasingly, however, the professional sports model has been one that promotes independence. Dr. Howard Katz, a psychiatrist and psychoanalyst, has said, "I think we are seeing individual aggrandizement becoming more important than subjugating oneself for the team. I think we have to realize that some of this comes from sports itself. Teams utilize competition among members as a motivational force; players are competing among themselves for space and time before they compete against other teams. Aggressiveness is a major tool. There seems to be a progressive movement in pro sports of going over the boundaries, and then the field is no longer a safe place for aggressive energy."[11]

For example, before the Phil Jackson era in Los Angeles, the Lakers had a running drama going between Coach Del Harris and point guard Nick Van Exel, neither one of whom wanted to cooperate with the other (both ended up getting booted from the team). After Jackson took over, another controversy erupted between Kobe Bryant and Shaquille O'Neal, both of whom wanted to be thought of as the Lakers' "go-to" guy. (Eventually, however, Bryant and O'Neal were able to see the value of cooperating with each other and with their coach to work toward their shared goal of winning an NBA championship.)

The danger is when we see this "me-first" attitude reflected in youth sports. It is very easy for the aggressiveness that putting your interests first spawns to turn into savagery. There have been numerous instances, for example, of parents attacking coaches, officials, and even other players in their zeal to see their child take his or her "rightful" place on the sports pedestal. (Remember the incident of the dad who sharpened his son's chin guard, thus inflicting several painful slices on the opposing players?)

Because sport is so prevalent in our lives, it has tremendous power for influencing how we think. How often, for example, have you heard life referred to as a game? I've done it myself many times. But the inference here is that some are going to win at life and some are going to lose—and that everybody is competing against everybody else.

Well, that's simply not true. The majority of life is about cooperation, not competition. Anyone who sees it differently is going to face a lot of problems in his or her life, and not just on the athletic field.

In conclusion, I would like to share a story of how two sports figures went from enemies to friends. There is a lesson here for all of us on the importance of cooperation.

In 1996, Roberto Alomar and John Hirschbeck became forever linked in the annals of baseball history when Alomar spit in Hirschbeck's face after an argument near home plate at Toronto's SkyDome. Alomar made matters worse afterward by saying he thought the umpire's behavior had been related to the stress of the death of his eight-year-old son, John Drew, who had died a few years earlier of a rare brain disease.

Afterward, Hirschbeck went out of his way to avoid Alomar. However, since Hirschbeck was a major-league umpire and Alomar was a major-league player, it was difficult. Finally, Hirschbeck went to a mutual friend. "What kind of a guy is Alomar?" Hirschbeck asked.

"He's one of the two nicest people I've ever met. And you're the other one."

That answer surprised Hirschbeck. Finally, he decided life was too short to go through it hating people. He approached Alomar and the two men decided it was time to let go of the past. They now consider each other friends. "If that's the worst thing Robbie ever does in his life, he'll lead a real good life," Hirschbeck said. "People make mistakes. You forgive, you forget, and you move on."[12]

Cooperating with others is seldom an easy thing to do, especially in the world of sports, where heightened feelings and intense pressure sometimes bring out the worst in people. However, as John Hirschbeck and Roberto Alomar prove, it is possible for enemies to become friends, and for individuals in the worst of circumstances to look beyond those circumstances to achieve a greater good.

So remember, as you work with your children to encourage cooperative behavior—if we want our kids to live in a world where people aren't just seeking to make a name for themselves but are genuinely interested in building more caring, productive communities, there is no better way to place them on the path to such a future than to get them thinking about cooperating on the field, the court, the track, and so on. We've seen how much people can accomplish in times of tragedy when they all pull together. Just think of how much our children's generation will be able to accomplish if this cooperative spirit is a part of their everyday life.

MODEL—TEACH—ENCOURAGE

1. Make sure your children understand what kind of cooperative behavior you expect from them. Give them specific examples (i.e., "I expect you to cheer for *all* of your teammates, not just your best friends").

2. Start a reward system where you reward them for their cooperative behavior. For example, if you have a child who is a basketball player, you could keep track of how many times he or she passes the ball, and go out for ice cream together whenever your child reaches a total of fifty passes.

3. Remember that negative methods (yelling, nagging, demanding) of trying to enlist your children's cooperation don't usually work.

4. Monitor your children's coaches to see if they reward athletes for cooperative behavior or uncooperative behavior.

5. Avoid power struggles. Work with your children to establish family rules and limits, and make sure these are clearly understood.

6. Help your younger children label and verbalize their feelings and the feelings of others.

7. Don't let your children use "But it wasn't fair!" to excuse poor behavior after a bad call.

8. Encourage family cooperation versus family competition. For example, one family had young children who loved it when the family went to the park to play Frisbee. However, kids being kids, the Frisbee toss often deteriorated into a competition of "let's see how hard I can make it for the other person to catch!" No one had much fun doing that. Then the parents said, "Let's see how many tosses we can make without dropping it."

9. Help your children sharpen their problem-solving skills by presenting them with problems (your daily newspaper can provide you with plenty of examples) and asking them how they would solve them.
10. Provide regular opportunities for children to develop productive and sustained friendships. For example, help them get to know their teammates better by arranging times for them to get together to play or practice. Acknowledge your children's efforts to initiate social interactions in appropriate ways.

A Good Sport Shows Integrity

*The important choices we make in our lives are never clear-cut.
There are good reasons in many situations to go one way or another.
Yet the ability to choose wisely or correctly is so fundamental to
building success, to exhibiting true leadership, that it sometimes
seems as if we are being asked to walk a high wire without a net
below us.*

—BILL RUSSELL[1]

*Bill Walton came to my office one afternoon at Pauley Pavilion with
a serious question for me. His knees had been causing him increasing pain over the last several months, to a point where it was obvious to anyone watching him play that just running the length of the
court hurt him badly.*

*"Coach," he said, "I've heard that smoking marijuana will reduce
the pain in my knees. Is it okay with you if I use it?"*

*I looked up from my desk and replied, "Bill, I haven't heard that
it is a pain reliever, but I have heard that it is illegal."*

—JOHN WOODEN, *WOODEN*[2]

During the summer of 2000, the competition that had everyone
holding his or her breath in anticipation wasn't Marion Jones's

quest for five gold medals at the Sidney Olympics. No, *this* competition centered around sixteen people stranded on a remote
island off the coast of Borneo. By day, they competed in various
contests designed to test their physical and mental skills. At
night—one by one—their companions voted them off the island,
until only one "survivor" remained. The million-dollar "Survivor"
prize was won by Richard Hatch, a corporate trainer whose
scheming and manipulative behavior led him to be known as "the
man 'Survivor' fans loved to hate."

What was it about Richard that drew so many people's ire?
After all, he was quite open about his tactics. He made it clear that
he had not come to the island to make friends, he had come to
play a game. While Sean was making speeches about taking the
higher ground, and Colleen was admonishing people to "be nice
and play fair," and Kelly was waffling back and forth about stab-
bing her so-called friends in the back, Richard simply did what he
had to do to win the game. In the process, he provided the audi-
ence with great entertainment.

I think one of the reasons people didn't want Richard to win
is that, deep down, most of us like our champions to be people
of integrity. Mark Burnett, executive producer of the show, wrote
that as the competition became more cutthroat even the pro-
duction crew began to feel uneasy. "To an individual, the crew
were repulsed that the game had reached a new moral low. Inher-
ent in their initial attraction to the project was the chance to see
greatness shine in humanity. A survivor should be someone
superlative for all the right reasons. Like the U.S. Olympic Hockey
team beating the Russians in 1980, Kirk Gibson hitting the impos-
sible home run in the 1988 World Series, and Dan Jansen finally
winning his Olympic gold after years of failure, the hope was that
the winner of "Survivor" would touch that wondrous core essence
of humanity. That the game was going in another direction was

mildly distressing, like a mirror reflecting poorly on the crew's own humanity."[3]

The ultimate message of "Survivor," however, was "Do what you have to in order to win, and you will be rewarded." Yes, it was entertainment—just as sport is entertainment. But it was entertainment that, like sports, sometimes left us feeling just a little bit icky.

Examining Your Integrity

"Survivor" held up a mirror that reflected poorly on how we, as people, sometimes play our games. So, too, does sport provide us with some thought-provoking reflections. For instance, how do you feel when you're watching your child's game and you see the other team get away with committing an obvious foul? Are you outraged? Upset? Angry at the unfairness of it all? You are probably all of these things, and more.

Now, how do you feel when you see your child commit a foul and get away with it? Do you jump out of your seat and shout, "Hey, ref! Are you blind? Didn't you see that foul? Throw that kid out of the game!" Or do you think, "Whew! We really dodged a bullet on that one!"

Adults are quick to jump on other people's lack of integrity, but when it comes to ourselves we can be just as quick to justify the lapses. "Hey, that's the way the world is," we say. "If you wanna compete, you've got to be prepared to do what it takes. Otherwise, you're going to get left behind." No wonder children get confused when they hear grown-ups talking about integrity at the same time they're cheating on their spouses, fudging their tax records, and padding their expense accounts.

Defining Integrity

When you hear the word *integrity*, what do you think of? I think of someone who is honest and who sticks to his or her principles. I also think of someone who is consistent—who not only sets high standards for himself or herself but who lives up to those standards even when faced with hard choices, choices that may be clouded by stress, pressure to succeed, or temptation. I think of someone like golfer Barclay Howard.

Howard, playing in his first U.S. Amateur Championship, could have kept his mouth shut and no one would have known. But the Scotland native discovered that he had accidentally played with two different styles of balls, breaking the one-ball rule. (The regulation is designed to prevent players from changing types of balls during a round.) So he went to the United States Golf Association president and had himself disqualified from the competition.

"I would know," said Howard when asked if anyone could have found out. "Say I was walking up to win on this weekend, how could I live with myself? After forty-four years, you're going to start cheating? No."

Howard didn't intentionally break the rule. He thought there was only one type of ball in his bag. He thought all the others had been emptied out. It was only after he played the round, signed his scorecard, and was about to give the ball back to his caddy that he noticed the error. At forty-four, and on the verge of qualifying for his first U.S. Amateur, knowing he might never get another chance, he disqualified himself. For him, winning was not as important as his personal integrity.[4]

As Barclay Howard illustrates, integrity doesn't come cheap. Integrity is hard work. It involves doing some serious thinking to determine what your values and priorities are. It involves continually reassessing those values and priorities to make sure that they are still relevant to one's life. Finally, it involves maintaining those values and priorities in day-to-day situations.

Few people really take the time to conduct the kind of self-examination needed to determine where they stand on matters of integrity. Why? For adults, there are simply not enough hours in the day to do everything we need to do, let alone fit in time for the kind of reflection and self-assessment that determining one's values requires. Children, on the other hand (especially younger ones) haven't really learned how to do this kind of introspective exercise yet. But I think the biggest reason is that most of us—no matter what our age—think we already know what our values and priorities are. It's not until we're put into a situation where we're unexpectedly challenged that we realize we don't know those things after all. And because we're not prepared, we end up making decisions or choices that might not be the best ones for us.

The Challenge of Teaching Integrity

Of all the actions of a good sport, integrity is probably the most difficult one to teach, and even more difficult to teach for transfer—that is, to help your children see that the integrity they show in their sport can and should be shown in the classroom, the workplace, and in their relationships.

In sport, it is usually easy to know what is right and what is wrong. The rules are clearly posted and the consequences are fairly obvious. Thus, you can say to your child, "In football, you're not allowed to spear an opponent because you could seriously injure that person or yourself."

But then you come to the gray areas. Areas like, what should your child do when a rule (such as that of palming the basketball while dribbling) is commonly ignored? What should he or she do when a teammate is competing for the same position, and that teammate asks for your child's help? What should your child do if he or she knows a teammate is taking steroids?

In life, the rules are not always clear. And the consequences are not always obvious. To succeed in today's world requires a kind of flexibility and adaptability that can make maintaining one's integrity difficult. That is why it is so important that parents take advantage of the opportunities that sport offers to help children learn lessons of integrity while they are young.

Christina Hoff Sommers, an associate professor of philosophy at Clark University, argues that part of the difficulty in teaching integrity is that too much of our focus these days is on social policy, or "public" morality (abortion, euthanasia, capital punishment, etc.), with not enough attention being paid to private morality (decency, honesty, honor, and personal responsibility).

> So many students come to college dogmatically committed to a moral relativism that offers them no grounds to think that cheating is just wrong. I sometimes play a macabre game with first-year students, trying to find some act they will condemn as morally wrong: Torturing a child. Starving someone to death. Humiliating an individual in a nursing home. The reply is often: "Torture, starvation, and humiliation may be bad for you or me, but who are we to say they are bad for someone else?" . . . A Harvard University professor annually offers a large history class on the Second World War and the rise of the Nazis. Some years back, he was stunned to learn from his teaching assistant that the majority of students in the class did not believe that anyone was really to blame for the Holocaust. The graduate assistant asserted that if these Harvard students were sitting in judgment at Nuremberg they would have let everyone off. No one was to blame. In the students' minds, the Holocaust was like a natural cataclysm: it was inevitable and

unavoidable. The professor refers to his students' attitude about the past as "no-fault history."[5]

I remember a time in my life when I had a similar attitude. As a young husband with problems in my marriage, I took the easy way out. Instead of facing up to my share of the responsibility in making the marriage work (which would have entailed a lot of painful self-examination and hard work), I chose to ignore the part I played in the dissolution of my marriage and believed that divorce was inevitable and unavoidable. In sport you hear a lot of talk about athletes needing to "check their egos at the door." I have come to believe that integrity demands we do just that. But at that stage in my life, I valued my ego more than the commitments I had made. To say that no one was at fault, that it was just "one of those things," meant that I didn't have to admit that, yes, there *were* faults, and some of them were mine. I have never stopped feeling the pain and guilt of that unnecessary and impulsive choice.

Now that I am in the fourth and final period of my life, I make a point to stay in daily contact with my values and ideals. As a result, I am making better decisions about those things that are important to me.

The point is, we usually know what the right thing is. To give up the right thing for something less than the ideal usually means a loss—in this case, not necessarily the loss of a game, but of an important human victory. In choosing to place winning or status over integrity, an athlete loses the battle over selfishness, ego, and taking the easy way out.

To help your children understand how important integrity is, you need to help them understand that any time an athletic competition is corrupted because of unethical actions, athletes are the ones who lose out. That's because there are consequences to dishonesty, cheating, and similar actions. These consequences include:

1. Lowered self-esteem (knowing you didn't accomplish something through your own efforts).
2. More loss of integrity (a cheater who doesn't get caught the first time usually cheats again because it seems easier).
3. Bigger problems in the future (making ethical decisions is a critical part of avoiding future problems).

On the other hand, athletes who exhibit integrity in their play—who choose to be honest with themselves and others, who respect and adhere to the rules of the game, and who take responsibility for their actions—will have the kind of self-esteem and strength of character that will help them make good and wise decisions throughout their lives.

Being Honest with Yourself and Others

How do we teach our children honesty? I think the most crucial point to get across to our kids is that dishonesty always comes with a price tag. When people lie, cheat, steal, or violate other ethical standards, they not only feel disappointed and ashamed of themselves, but their lack of integrity also affects their relationships with others. Trust is essential in any important relationship. Who can trust someone who is dishonest or unfair?

For most people, dishonesty causes guilt, remorse, or at the least, a twinge of conscience. It has a corrosive quality that eats away at you, whether you're five or fifty.

One major-league manager who used to enthrall his players with stories of his adventures in Vietnam with the U.S. Marines experienced this corrosiveness firsthand. The truth was he had never actually seen combat in Vietnam. His military time had been spent in the marine reserves. This man's lies caused him many sleepless nights and, once the story got out, became an embarrassment and distraction to his team.

The pressure of sports competition combined with the emphasis on winning often leads individuals to say things or make decisions that they normally wouldn't. I remember in one of my pickup basketball games I was trying to block an opponent's shot and he pushed my hand away—a clearly illegal maneuver. When I called him on it (we call our own fouls in these games), another player on his team who was not in a position to see what had happened loudly challenged my call. It was an uncomfortable situation, not just because the one player was challenging my integrity, but also because the teammate who committed the foul should have taken the responsibility of calling the foul on himself in the first place. One person's lack of integrity (and another person's lack of tact) ended up interrupting the flow and enjoyment of the game for all of us.

A similar, but much more serious incident occurred during the NCAA semifinals a few years ago. North Carolina senior center Makhtar Ndiaye accused Utah's Britton Johnsen of using a racial epithet during North Carolina's loss to Utah. Johnsen flatly denied the accusation. Later, Ndiaye admitted that he had lied about the incident—that the pressure of the game and some rough contact with Johnsen had led him to say what he did.

Then there was the matter of Notre Dame's coach-for-a-week George O'Leary, who hadn't even had time to unpack before the Fighting Irish discovered that their newly hired coach's résumé contained several inaccuracies—for instance, he didn't really have a master's degree, and he had never actually lettered in college football.

Again, it is a matter of getting so caught up in wanting to win (or to at least look good) that it overpowers everything else. It happens on the court. It happens in the classroom. It can happen anywhere.

Impress upon your children that dishonest actions like these leave a bad taste in the mouth of everyone involved—players, coaches, and spectators alike. They are not the actions of a good sport, and they do not help to create a sports environment that uplifts or inspires. Whether your children are hearing about professional athletes taking banned drugs, corking their bats, and greasing their jerseys, or listening to you lecture them about not drinking or smoking and then watching you do those very same things, it sends a message about honesty and integrity in sports and in life. That message is that integrity is a matter of convenience.

Sport is a perfect tool for teaching children not just the value of integrity, but how they can act in order to be a person of integrity. But it is up to you to help your children learn these things. They're not going to lie in their beds at night and reflect on what integrity means to them. They're too busy dreaming about pitching no-hitters and scoring the winning goal.

This means that not only do you have a responsibility to set an example that your children can follow, you also have a responsibility to help your children recognize what their own values are and prepare for situations where those values may be tested. What are some ways you can do this?

- Teach your children to weigh their decisions carefully by asking themselves, "How will this action affect me and others? Will it be helpful or hurtful? How would I feel if anyone could see me doing this?" (If they would rather hide their actions, it's a good indication that they're doing something wrong.)
- Encourage your children to think about what they would do in an ethical situation. For example, what would they do if they saw a teammate cheating, or if they were encouraged by

a teammate or coach to cheat? Help them plan their strategy ahead of time for what they might do to handle the situation.

- Remember that children are focused on the here and now. Help your children look beyond the short-term reward for lying or cheating (no punishment, winning a game, etc.) to the long-term consequences of their actions (unfair blame on someone else, damage to personal relationships, erosion of self-esteem, etc.).

Respecting the Rules of the Game

If you're a pro, then you often don't decide whether to cheat based on if it's "right or wrong"; you base it on whether you can get away with it.

—Former Brewers manager George Bamberger[6]

Most NFL players occasionally break the rules the way that most people break the speed limit. . . . In football, you're not wrong unless you're caught.

—Tim Green, former Atlanta Falcon[7]

The second aspect of integrity you need to discuss with your children is respecting the rules. To me, respecting the rules means playing by the rules.

Why is it important for athletes to play by the rules? For one, it's a life lesson. Because pretty much everything in life is governed by rules, if you want to get along in life, you need to abide by these rules.

Athletes should play by the rules because they love the game, and because they recognize that without rules the game would eventually be destroyed. They should also play by the rules because they love themselves—and cheating chips away at that self-love.

When winning becomes more important to your child's self-esteem than respecting the rules, then you are going to have problems. This problem was aptly detailed in a 1997 *Sports Illustrated* article profiling the issue of drug use in Olympic athletes:

> A scenario, from a 1995 poll of 198 sprinters, swimmers, power-lifters and other assorted athletes, most of them U.S. Olympians or aspiring Olympians: You are offered a banned performance-enhancing substance, with two guarantees: 1) You will not be caught. 2) You will win. Would you take the substance?
>
> One hundred and ninety-five athletes said yes; three said no.
>
> Scenario II: You are offered a banned performance-enhancing substance that comes with two guarantees: 1) You will not be caught. 2) You will win every competition you enter for the next five years, and then you will die from the side effects of the substance. Would you take it?
>
> More than half the athletes said yes.[8]

This *Sports Illustrated* article is disturbing for many reasons, two of which are the importance that winning holds in the lives of these athletes, and the fact that *if they knew they would not get caught*, the overwhelming majority would cheat. You see, to be a person of integrity doesn't just mean that you respect the rules when all eyes are upon you; it means you respect the rules even when no one is watching.

I think one reason many of today's athletes show so little respect for the rules is that they know little about the games they are playing. How much do your children know about their favorite sports? Do they know who invented them? Do they know how the game was originally played? Do they know how the rules have changed over the years, and why?

I have had veterans of wars tell me how painful it is to them when they see young people failing to show our country's flag its proper respect. And I have had those same young people tell me that they have gained new respect for the flag after studying its history and hearing the stories of those individuals who sacrificed their lives for what the flag stands for.

It is the same way with sport. When you teach your children the history of the game, you are also teaching them to respect the rules of that game. You are teaching them that the rules are there for a reason. You are teaching them that rules make the contest fair and safe for everyone.

One danger of disregarding the rules is that it can lead your children to view their opponents as objects rather than human beings. Seeing people as objects leads us to use people for our own ends rather than to approach them as partners in the sports experience. To this day, some of my best friends are people I competed against in high school and college. Would I have been able to say the same if I had seen these individuals as "the enemy" rather than my compatriots in a shared adventure?

Another dangerous consequence of breaking the rules is that it can lead your children to develop "moral calluses." Moral calluses keep us from feeling right and wrong. Every time we rationalize breaking a rule ("No one's gonna know," "It was just a little thing," "Everybody does it") we add another layer to the callus. The more layers, the harder it becomes to feel the pricks of conscience.

It can be especially hard for your children to feel the prick of their conscience when faced with a situation where following the rules isn't clearly black or white. The question of what is sound strategy and what is moral trickery is one that has long been debated in sports. In some games, such as football and basketball, certain kinds of cheating have become an ordinary and accepted part of the game. It is considered part of "technique." The rationale is it's okay to cheat as long as you're subtle about it. For exam-

ple, not long after Michael Jordan became head of basketball oper-
ations for the Washington Wizards, a newspaper reporter
described an incident where Jordan was showing one of the team's
rookies some of the "tricks" of the game. This prompted an angry
letter to the editor by a reader who didn't appreciate a hero to children such as Jordan showing how to cheat and get away with it.

Baseball players are also notorious for what they try to get away
with during a game. One old-time baseball player, King Kelly, took
advantage of the fact that there used to be only one umpire by
skipping second base in his run from first to third. More recently,
Amos Otis admitted to using a corked bat throughout his
thirteen-year career with the Kansas City Royals. "I did what it
took for me to stay in the major leagues. I never got caught, so I
never had any reason to feel guilty."[9]

We sometimes smile at stories like these, but should we? In particular, you have to ask yourself, "What *are* the implications of
adults teaching children how to cheat and get away with it?" If you
truly believe that sport is preparing your children for life, then can
you blink at cheating in sports and not expect the lesson to carry
over?

I'm not talking about merely stretching the rules. Athletes will
routinely test officials to see how closely they will call a particular game. But cheating is something else again—it is the deliber-
ate violation of rules for personal advantage while trying to avoid
detection. How much more ethical is it for coaches—especially
adults who are coaching children—to counsel athletes in the techniques of holding, hooking, flopping, and otherwise attempting
to deceive those whose job it is to enforce the rules?

This was one of the issues that came up at a conference on
sportsmanship sponsored by Character Counts! Sports, the California Interscholastic Federation, and California State University—Long Beach. The subject was "pursuing victory with honor."
At the conference, panelists were asked to probe the concepts of

honor, ethics, and sportsmanship in the context of specific questions about techniques and practices including legalistic evasions of recruiting and eligibility rules, equipment tampering, altering the field of play, taunting and trash talking, tactical arguing with officials, deceptions to induce an erroneous call, intentional fouls, fake time-outs, etc.

One of the questions debated at the conference was, "What is cheating as opposed to smart play?" Apparently many coaches—especially those in the professional ranks—have the attitude "if you aren't cheating, you aren't trying." Kathy Marpe, women's basketball coach for the University of San Diego, admitted that, even though she believes it is wrong, she has coached her team in the methods of knocking an opposing shooter on the arm in a way that is difficult for referees to detect. "Because if I want to compete then I have to," Marpe explained.[10]

I feel fortunate that I played sports in an era when the culture of sport was about winning fairly on the playing field and not through bending the rules. That doesn't mean that athletes didn't ever break a rule when I played. It still happened. But more often than not, when we would break a rule we weren't hoping that we *wouldn't* get caught—we were hoping we *would* get caught.

In my book *Court Sense: The Invisible Edge in Basketball and Life*, I talk more about the importance of knowing the rules thoroughly—not just so that you don't unwittingly break them, but also so that you know when *to* break them. In this case, I am talking about those instances when a player or coach breaks a rule in order to use the penalty to his or her advantage. This, to me, is strategic playing.

Paul Westphal, in the days when he was playing for the Phoenix Suns, executed a perfect example of this kind of strategy. It was the 1976 NBA finals, and the Suns were playing the Boston Celtics. The Celtics were ahead with less than ten seconds to play, and Westphal, the Suns' star point guard, was on the bench. Phoenix was out of time-outs, and Westphal knew it. Still, he told the head coach, Cotton Fitzsimmons, to call one anyway. It took Fitzsimmons a few seconds to figure out what Westphal was thinking. Then he realized that if Phoenix called a time-out, Boston would gain possession after a single free-throw attempt and have to inbound the ball, which Phoenix might be able to intercept. Even if Boston made the free throw (which they did), they would only have a two-point lead. If Phoenix could gain possession on the inbound pass and score, it might force the game into overtime.

That's exactly what happened. Boston did go on to win in overtime, but the strategy gave Phoenix a second chance. It's similar to the way a football team about to kick a field goal will sometimes choose to receive a delay-of-game penalty in order to give the kicker better field position.

What we are actually talking about here is situational ethics. Sometimes in life we are put in situations where we feel that we need to break a rule or go against our values for a greater good. In World War II, Dietrich Bonhoeffer, a German pastor and ethics professor, participated in a plot to assassinate Hitler, even though he believed that it was wrong to kill. Corrie ten Boom fervently believed that it was wrong to lie or steal, but she lied to German authorities and didn't think twice about stealing identification papers as she worked to save hundreds of Jewish people in Holland.

At the same time, there were devoutly religious people in Germany and Holland (and other places) who would not have killed Hitler if given the chance, and who believed that it was not right to lie or steal to save your neighbors. Were they necessarily wrong in their values? No, they weren't. Every person has to make his or her own decisions as to what is right for him or her to do in any given situation.

You need to help your children understand and prepare for those times when they will experience the "situational ethics" of sports. Even when they choose to purposely break a rule in order to use the penalty to their advantage, your children will still run into gray areas where they have to ask themselves, "Should I do this or not?" Making a decision that is right for them requires having a solid grounding in personal integrity.

This means helping your children avoid the "everybody does it" cop-out by getting them to consider "You are not everybody. You are your own person. What is it that *you* want from sport? Do you want to be able to walk away knowing that you played a clean game? Do you want to be someone who lowers his or her standard to the lowest common denominator? Or do you want to be someone who sets the standard for everyone else?" Your children may not know the answer to these questions, or they may not answer them the way you want them to. But by asking these questions, you have planted the seed, and challenged them to think about what they would do in circumstances that test their integrity.

At the same time, parents have their own questions to ask. In the 1999 women's World Cup, goalkeeper Brianna Scurry admitted to stepping into an illegal area during the sudden-death shootout on the save that helped win the game for the U.S. team. In other words, she admitted to cheating to win. The rationale behind her action was, "It's a stupid rule, everyone agrees it's a stupid rule, all the other goalkeepers do it, and I didn't get called for it. No call, no foul."

From your point of view, was this a brilliant piece of strategy or another distressing example of the moral inconsistency of professional sports?

What *should* an athlete do in those circumstances where a rule doesn't make much sense, or seems unfair? Take the issue of eligibility, for example. Eligibility rules exist to help keep one team from having an unfair advantage over another. However, there are few rules that are as universally despised. To coaches, eligibility rules are a major headache. To parents and athletes, they are seen as stumbling blocks that can get in the way of an athlete's opportunity for fame and fortune.

No wonder, then, that some coaches, parents, and athletes manage to find numerous ways to skirt the eligibility rules. Parents have lied about residency and legal guardianship. Some have falsified birth certificates, or held their children back a grade to give them physical advantages in sport later. Schools routinely deny they recruit, but nonetheless, many talented prep athletes move from school to school to play on high-profile teams in the hope of making themselves more marketable to college recruiters. Players receive credit for courses they did not pass, in order to stay eligible.

When a rule is unfair or doesn't seem to make sense, parents and athletes have three choices. One, they can break the rule. Two, they can seek to change the rule. Or, three, they can follow the rule.

Under the old sportsmanship, following the rules would entail following the letter of the rule. Under the new sportsmanship, it entails following the spirit of the rules, not just the letter. The spirit of the eligibility rules implies that if players of varying skill levels are distributed within and between each set of teams, a more fair and equitable competitive playing field should occur.[11] As the authors of *Sports Ethics* caution, "Unless individuals in sport value the full application of the rules, more and more rules will have to be written and enforced to close the loopholes currently being exploited to someone's advantage. . . . Rather than matching opponents' talents and strategies, too many games lapse into players and coaches seeking to gain advantages without being penalized."[12]

Ultimately, you cannot write a rule to cover every situation. And an athlete can follow a rule to its letter and still be guilty of unsportsmanlike behavior. That is why you must help your children look beyond the rules and beyond the standard of what everybody else is doing to seeing sport as not just a contest to be won or lost, but as a step in the process of becoming a more complete person.

Being Responsible

You can make mistakes, but you aren't a failure until you start blaming others for those mistakes.

—JOHN WOODEN[13]

Recent research with more than 35,000 sport participants, from ninth-graders through university students, found that the longer individuals participate in sport, the more morally callused they become; that is, the less they respect their opponents and teammates or take into account honesty, justice, and the letter and spirit of the rules. . . . the reality of sport today, on analysis of the competitive model, does not support the concept of being responsible, honest, fair, or concerned for others.

—LUMPKIN, STOLL, AND BELLER, SPORTS ETHICS[14]

A friend of mine told me an interesting story recently. She was talking with her mother-in-law about laundry (of all things) and the mother-in-law said one of the saddest days of her life was the day she had to insist that her three teenage children be responsible for doing their own laundry. "I just couldn't keep up with it anymore," the older woman explained. "I was working full-time and the kids were going through so many clothes that I finally had to put my foot down and make them help. But I cried afterwards."

"What in the world for?" my friend asked.

"Because I was the mom," her mother-in-law replied. "I felt it should be my job to take care of them."

As parents, it *is* our job to take care of our children. But it is also our job to teach them how to take care of themselves. It is our job to teach them to move from dependency to independence so that they can eventually become self-sufficient adults. That is called responsibility.

Responsibility means that, as a parent, you should never do for your kids on a regular basis what they are able to do for themselves. Responsibility means that kids should do what they are supposed to do, try to do their best, use self-control and self-discipline, think before they act, recognize and consider the consequences of their actions, and be accountable for their choices. In both cases, responsibility means recognizing that we are all interdependent upon one another. One person's actions almost always affect someone else.

In earlier days, people were more aware of this interdependence. In the agricultural society, large families were important because children were needed to help keep the farm and the household running. Communities pulled together to build barns, put out fires, and stop floods. Today, we don't need to rely on our children and each other as much. However, through sport, we can still teach our children the same basic principle of responsibility that our grandparents learned.

Responsibility isn't easy. It's a natural human tendency to want to avoid it. I have two grandsons, ages six and four. Whenever I ask them who is responsible for a particular piece of wrongdoing, it's never one of them. It's usually someone named "I don't know." (When I finally catch up to this "I don't know" person, is he going to get an earful!)

Even adults do this. During the second game of the 1998 American League championship series, Chuck Knoblauch decided that instead of retrieving a ball that was still in play (and just a few feet away from him), he was going to argue with the umpires about a bad call. His action may have cost the Yankees the game.

Afterward, Knoblauch defended his actions by saying that he didn't see the ball and that he wouldn't have done anything differently. Later, he confessed that he had seen the ball, but he was so intent on making the officials see his point of view that he just ignored it.

It is a sign of maturity to accept responsibility for one's actions. If you want to raise responsible athletes, you need to help your children recognize that they are accountable for what they do. They are accountable to their team, the coach, and the game. They have a responsibility to play to their best ability and to seek their highest competitive level.

Responsibility comes through learning how to make responsible decisions. Too often in sport and life, children are not given the opportunity to make their own decisions. As a counselor, many of the problems I have dealt with have come about because individuals did not learn how to make responsible decisions.

Decision making is a skill that we can begin teaching our children at an early age. Toddlers can choose whether they want juice or milk for dinner. Older children can choose what clothes they want to wear to school.

Of course, there is decision making, and there is *responsible* decision making. Teaching children how to make responsible decisions is a little more complicated. Often it involves letting them make mistakes—something that is hard for parents to do. One mom, in a hurry to pick up her five-year-old at school, told her three-year-old to put her coat on because it was chilly outside. The little girl refused. So the mom said, "Okay, you can choose not to wear your coat, but you're going to get cold and we won't be able to come back and get it." Sure enough, the little girl shivered and whined all the way to the school. She also learned an important lesson about consequences.

In her book *Champions Are Raised, Not Born*, Summer Sanders talks about the decision she made to give up her Stanford athletic scholarship after the 1992 Olympics. It turned out to be a difficult situation. She was traveling around the world doing speaking engagements and endorsement jobs, but she wasn't having much fun. She was no longer a part of the swimming team. She didn't have time for her friends. She learned that it wasn't possible to "have her cake and eat it, too."

> If the consequences of my eligibility decision were ones I didn't particularly like—and I regretted them terribly at the time—I nonetheless never felt I had the option to go back on my decision. I'd committed myself, and as a child of divorce, I'd grown up to view a broken commitment as the worst possible thing. My parents had broken their commitment to each other—an unforgivable thing. But I'll give them this: they accepted the consequences, the personal sacrifices, which came from that decision. Trevor and I always understood that having the freedom to choose meant paying the price of living through the consequences of your choice.[15]

When adults are the ones making all the moral and competitive judgments, it has a negative influence on a young athlete's moral growth as well as his or her personal development. When adult athletes (those in the college or professional ranks) are treated like small children—such as when college athletes are provided with "baby-sitters" who ensure that the athletes attend their classes—then they are failing to learn responsibility.

Athletes who receive special treatment from the time they are young grow into adults who believe that special treatment is their "right," that they don't have a responsibility to follow the same rules and guidelines that other people follow. For example, an eighteen-year-old basketball player in San Antonio was sentenced to five years in prison for elbowing an opponent during a game.

The incident happened after the play was finished and was away from the ball. The action left the victim with a concussion and a broken nose that required emergency surgery.

After the offending athlete was sentenced, one sportswriter objected to the punishment because he didn't feel that hitting another player during the course of a competition was illegal. Another sportswriter disagreed by saying, "That's just the kind of wrongheaded thinking that surrounds sports. Just listen to NHL player Paul Kariya explain why the police shouldn't be involved in the McSorley incident: 'We are our own entity. If we can't control what goes on in games, we have serious problems. If we get the police involved, what does that say about our league?' It says the league and sports aren't above the law. It says sports is not its own entity."[16]

In order to learn responsibility, young athletes need to have responsible role models. Ideally, those role models would be a parent or other family member. In reality, those role models are often professional athletes or others in the sports world, who don't always set the best examples.

One of my favorite examples of a positive sports role model is the college basketball coach who suspended himself for one game after he used profanity on a postgame radio show. As the father of a four-year-old daughter, he had been trying to cut down on his bad language in order to be a better example to her and other young fans. He had asked his players to watch their language, too. So when he let the word slip, he held himself accountable.[17]

At the other end of the spectrum, you have people like Bobby Knight. The scandal surrounding the infamous former Hoosier coach unfolded during the writing of this book. It began when a former player came forth with the allegation that Knight had once choked him during a practice—an allegation that Knight flat-out denied. Then a video turned up that showed the incident in question. Additional bad behavior by Knight then came to light. Through it all, Knight maintained an unrepentant manner, apologizing only when forced to, in the way that children often do when they are forced to apologize but really aren't sorry for anything. ("I've always been too confrontational, especially when I know I'm right.")

Finally, after breaking a "zero-tolerance" policy when he scolded a student who called him by his last name, Knight was fired. However, he continued his stance of nonresponsibility by saying no one had really explained to him what "zero tolerance" meant.

Since we are only human, there are times that we all fail to act in a responsible way. If you have not always been the most responsible person in the world, don't beat yourself up about it. But *do* resolve to do better. For example, after Atlanta's John Rocker made racist and antiforeigner statements to the press, sportswriter Bill Plaschke waited to see how Rocker would be received by the ethnically diverse Los Angeles Dodgers fans. In the eighth inning, when Rocker took the mound:

> The stadium rocked with boos and jeers, the most inspired anger here in years. Then out of the stands flew cups of beer, trash, and then some idiot who ran to second base and pulled down his pants.
>
> Although certainly he was no bigger idiot than I.
>
> Because while all this was happening, I was cheering. . . . I quickly wrote, and 15 minutes later filed, a story that applauded the fans not just for their booing, but for their pelting and pants dropping. I sat overlooking empty Dodger Stadium for a few moments with a contented smile. . . .
>
> Then, I gasped.
>
> And I thought, what have I just done?
>
> Applauded people for the same sort of intolerance for which Rocker stood accused?

Endorsed lawlessness?

Written something that I would be ashamed to show my children?

I quickly called the office and asked that the column be changed to include applause only for the boos, and boos for everything else. . . . There was only one problem. The presses had already started running. . . .

In applauding the fans for abusing John Rocker, I had been guilty of the same impulsive stupidity for which Rocker is now famous.[18]

Responsibility means having the courage to do the right thing. Most of us know what the right thing is, but not everyone has the courage to do it. At the U.S. Olympic trials for the new Olympic sport of tae kwon do, Kay Poe—the favorite—dislocated her knee in the semifinal match. Now it was time for the final match, and Poe, who could barely stand, was to face her friend, Esther Kim. Kim's father coached both girls. Kim had lost to Poe in an earlier round. Now she had a chance to win and earn the trip to Sidney. But it didn't feel right to her. So she forfeited the match, allowing her friend to be the one to go to the Olympics. "It felt like the only right thing to do," Kim told the *New York Times*. "It did hurt, but winning a gold medal isn't everything. There are other ways to be a champion."[19]

In my opinion, Esther Kim got it right. There is more to life than sport, and there is more to sport than sport. Responsible athletes will recognize that fact. Responsible parents will help them.

When Integrity Is Lost, Everyone Loses

Because we all have a common stake in creating good sports, the actions of each individual *do* matter. It is essential that athletes act with integrity in order to create the kind of sports community in which we all want to be a part. As a parent, you can help your children become athletes of integrity by setting an example that they can follow, actively looking for "teachable moments" to help them learn important principles and skills, and encouraging them to reflect upon their values and plan for situations in which those values might be challenged.

The integrity of sportsmanship has little to do with what society thinks and everything to do with what you and your child personally believe is the right thing to do. I remember hearing about a young baseball player who, after an umpire declared him "safe," admitted that he had not tagged the base. In effect, this young man ruled himself "out." While many people lauded the boy's honesty, there were others who felt that the boy should be faulted for contradicting the umpire's ruling.

The message that this sends to parents is that you cannot leave integrity up to chance, nor assume that your children will learn it from society. You need to actively work with your children to ensure that they have carefully considered the standards by which they want to live and play and compete. By doing this, you are laying the groundwork for your children to make decisions that they can be proud of throughout their lives.

MODEL—TEACH—ENCOURAGE

1. Encourage your children to see their competitors as individuals.
2. Don't overemphasize your children's sports victories. Be sure to praise sportsmanship more than achievement.
3. Emphasize honesty as a valued behavior in your family.

4. Set an example of truthfulness and honesty. Never ask your children to lie for you ("Tell him I'm not home"). Let your children see you go out of your way to be honest. Admit your own mistakes and let your children see how you rectify them.

5. Encourage honesty by being quicker to praise your children for their truthfulness than you are to punish them for lying.

6. With older children, discuss the concept of honesty. Talk about gray areas such as telling only part of the truth, cheating, lying to protect themselves or someone else, white lies, and so on.

7. Ask your children if they would want to be friends with someone who lies. Why or why not?

8. Sound out your children's coaches to get their feelings about such values as honesty, justice, and responsibility in sports.

9. If you coach your children, don't teach cheating—even if you're the only coach in the league who doesn't. Similarly, monitor your children's coaches to see if they are teaching unethical strategies to your children. If they are, be sure to explain to your children why you disagree with what the coach is doing, and discuss ways that they can achieve the same results without cheating.

10. Discuss with your children the importance of the rules and the "spirit" of the rules.

11. Remind your children that when they break a rule or a law, they are losing control over their life by giving others the power to impose a punishment.

12. Rather than teaching your children to ignore certain sports rules, teach them how to question and change rules and policies that are unjust, precipitate dishonest actions, or are irresponsible.

13. Help your children appreciate and value the history of their sport. This will also help them better appreciate the rules of the game.
14. Remind your children that winning is acceptable only if the letter and spirit of the rules are followed.
15. Don't make exceptions because of sport. In other words, don't do your children's homework or otherwise exempt your children from responsibility because of athletic demands. Too often the result of this is an irresponsible person who doesn't have the skills to succeed in anything in life except sport.
16. Give your children lots of positive feedback when they act responsibly.
17. Examine your own behavior and attitude toward fulfilling your responsibilities. Are you often late for things? Do you forget to follow through with assignments? Can people depend on you? Do you grumble about having to do things, or do you fulfill your responsibilities cheerfully?
18. Be consistent in your expectations. If you say you expect your children to wash their own uniforms, don't give in and do it for them.
19. Allow your children to experience the consequences of their actions. If your children are dawdling around instead of getting ready for practice, let them be late, even if it means being benched for a game.
20. Stay calm if you catch your children in unethical behavior. Flying off the handle encourages them to become defensive, rather than reflective. At the same time, establish consequences for misbehavior and stick to them.
21. Look for examples or stories of athletes that reinforce the standards you are trying to instill in your children.

A Good Sport Exhibits Self-Confidence

Swimming is a gift—my gift. It can't be about, "Kill the competitor." It's got to be, "I've trained hard. I've achieved my goals. Let's see how I can do."

It's got to be about the gratification of achieving and about making the most of it while I'm still physically able. Above all else, it's got to be about having the most fun that I can. Because that's when I truly feel like me.

—JENNY THOMPSON, OLYMPIC SWIMMER[1]

Self-confidence is a critical part of an athlete's ability to show sportsmanship at all times and in all circumstances. Self-confidence allows athletes to more easily get over their losses and move on. ("My opponent beat me today, but I don't need to throw a tantrum because I know I can do better next time.") It allows athletes to see themselves as more than just athletes. ("Just because I lost today doesn't mean I'm a failure as a person. I've still got lots of things to feel good about.") Self-confidence also allows athletes to have the courage to stand up for what is right. ("No, I don't think it's cool to scribble graffiti on the other team's gym, and if you guys do it, then I will tell the coach.")

As you can see, self-confidence is one of the most important things any of us can have—in or out of sports. Self-confidence reflects how we feel about ourselves. Self-confident athletes believe in themselves. They trust their own abilities and judgment, aren't easily swayed by others, and have a greater sense of control over their sports careers. On the other hand, athletes who are not self-confident find themselves depending excessively on the approval of others—parents, teammates, coaches, fans—in order to feel good about themselves. Instead of setting standards of sportsmanship, they follow the standards of those whose approval is most important to them.

Developing Self-Confidence

A friend of mine—an accomplished author—has said that the first time he set out to write a book, he was consumed with self-doubt. Would he be able to think of enough words? Would they make sense? Would anyone want to read them? Would anyone want to read them enough to pay for them? Even the act of saying to people, "Yes, I'm writing a book," seemed terribly grandiose and presumptuous—as if he were putting himself in the same category as Hemingway or Steinbeck.

But now, several books later, he thinks nothing of sitting down at his computer and starting a new manuscript. While he realizes he's still not in the same category as Hemingway or Steinbeck, he's become confident enough of his skills that he no longer thinks, "I wonder if this will sell," but rather, "I wonder how much this will sell for?"

Self-confidence is not something a child is born with. It is something that children develop. Albert Bandura—a psychology professor at Stanford back in the days when I was a student—did some pioneering work on the concept of self-efficacy, which is a situation-specific form of self-confidence (for example, a basketball player who makes a key three-point shot comes to believe that he or she can make three-point shots in a clutch situation).

Research suggests that a person's sense of self-efficacy, or confidence in a specific situation, leads to better performances. For instance, if that basketball player who believes he can make the three-point shot in clutch situations unexpectedly starts missing a lot of three-pointers, his sense of self-efficacy will spur him on to make a greater effort to overcome the challenge. He will be more likely to try a new way of shooting if the old one isn't working. He will have a greater commitment to getting out of his slump. He will have more confidence that he will be able to do so.

Bandura suggested that the way to increase self-efficacy is to:

- Begin with small steps that produce positive results versus the all-or-nothing, sink-or-swim approach.
- Try to emulate others. When I was a kid I loved to go to a college or pro game and then come home and spend hours practicing what I had witnessed.
- See nervous energy in a positive light. Some people get nervous and the butterflies undermine their performance. On the other hand, I always liked the sensation of having butterflies in my stomach. It made me more alert and eager to get into action.
- Use positive self-talk. When I was a young athlete, "self-talk" wasn't a term that we were familiar with. But we did know that thinking you could do something was a lot more likely to improve your performance than thinking you *couldn't* do it.

In sport, an athlete's self-confidence comes from having a realistic expectation of success based on well-practiced physical skills, a good knowledge of the sport, respect for his or her own competence, adequate preparation, and good physical condition. When I was in elementary school and junior high, I used to shoot hundreds of baskets each day before school. The hard work and preparation I put in gave me confidence in my ability. I knew that I could realistically expect to succeed when it came time to make a shot. Some athletes rely less on hard work and more on their natural talent to give them confidence. That's nice if you have that kind of talent, but most athletes don't. Hard work and preparation, on the other hand, is something that everyone can do.

Athletes can also gain confidence from measuring their success in terms of how well they do on their personal performance goals instead of how well they do on achievement goals such as winning. As Olympic medal winner Summer Sanders noted, it wasn't winning that gave her confidence. It was setting challenges and mastering them.[2]

Self-confidence also grows when athletes enjoy what they are doing. Jenny Thompson's outstanding performance in Sydney in 2000—which helped her accumulate more gold medals than any other U.S. woman in history—was one of the feel-good stories of the Olympics. But Thompson didn't always feel so good about herself.

Thompson (whose gold medals have all come in relays) had been expected to be a big contender for an individual gold medal at the 1996 Olympics in Atlanta. Instead, she choked at the trials and didn't qualify for a single individual event. The experience was devastating for her. However, despite the unexpected setback, Thompson went on to anchor three gold-winning relays at Atlanta, and to win both individual (bronze) and relay (gold) medals in Sydney.

How was Thompson able to shake off her failure in the trials to come back and swim confidently in the relays? She had help from Richard Diana, a performance-enhancement specialist who was working with several members of the U.S. women's team.

Diana's theory was that athletes performed best when they were in their "original state," or that state of being where they felt most calm and aware of themselves. It was Diana's opinion that Jenny Thompson was a naturally caring and compassionate person. By focusing on the joy of competition—the aura and excitement—rather than focusing on vanquishing her opponents, then she'd be in her original state.[3]

What Diana told Thompson to do was to go back to what she loved about swimming as a child. In other words, she had to learn to relax and enjoy the experience—to "live in the moment"—in order to swim better and feel more confident.

Self-confidence not only made sport "good" again for Jenny Thompson; it helped her become a better sport. It helped her be the kind of person who could wholeheartedly support her teammates, instead of moaning about what she was missing. It helped her see that swimming was only one area of her life, and that not living up to expectations in that area didn't mean she was a failure everywhere.

Another way athletes develop confidence is through the influence of significant others. When athletes receive compliments and praise from their coaches, families, friends, and so on, it is not just an ego boost, but a confidence boost. That's why you should always try to speak to your children in ways that build their self-esteem and help them feel positive about themselves—even when you're criticizing them. As Elizabeth Pantley suggests, "Point out what you *want to see* rather than what you *don't want to see*."[4] Pantley illustrates this principle with the following example:

Jimmy Johnson, the renowned former coach of the Dallas Cowboys, used this technique with his players. He was known for saying, "Protect the ball" (instead of "Don't fumble") or "Make this one" (instead of "Don't miss it"). His post-game meetings focused his players' thoughts forward to "how we can win the next game," instead of rehashing a loss. Under Johnson's positive leadership, the Cowboys won the Super Bowl in 1993 and 1994.[5]

Whether he realized it or not, Jimmy Johnson was teaching his players a basic tenet of sportsmanship—that sportsmanship means focusing on the positive, not the negative, of sports. Confident players are more likely to focus on the positive.

As a parent, you can help instill confidence in your children by following Johnson's example. Encourage your children with positive words, rather than discourage them with negative ones. At the same time, you need to be watchful that they don't rely too much on what you—or anyone else—says in order to feel a sense of confidence. Ultimately, self-confidence must come from within, not from without.

You also need to watch your children to make sure they don't fall into one of these other confidence-busting traps:

• **Confidence buster: thinking you need to be perfect.** Not only is this an unattainable goal, it also suggests that personal worth is determined by achievement. Children who think they need to be perfect as athletes tend to overreact when their performance falls short, resulting in displays of poor sportsmanship. I remember as a counselor working with a young high school pitcher who was a big perfectionist. Any time he had a bad game or a bad inning, he would pout and sulk and sit around making negative comments to his teammates. Because this young man's goals were irrational and unrealistic, he experienced great discomfort and stress every time he played. At one point he was ready to give up baseball.

To help this young man, I used a technique called *cognitive restructuring*. This is a method of teaching people that what they feel is the result of how they view a situation—meaning if you can change your viewpoint, you can change your feelings. I helped this young man see that success is a roller coaster, with daily ups and downs. I also helped him realize that mistakes can be teachers and are a natural aspect of growing and developing as a human being. Ultimately, he learned that his perfectionism was irrational and that he, like all accomplished athletes, would continue to experience fluctuations on the road to excellence. With additional assistance from his coach and his parents, who reassured him that they would still love him regardless of his performance, he came to accept the reality of setbacks as normal to the game and as springboards to further improvement. He went on to win a scholarship to a Division I school and later signed a professional baseball contract.

• **Confidence buster: dwelling on the past.** Not only is it harmful to dwell on mistakes you have made in the past, it is also harmful to dwell on the mistakes of others. Young athletes can get equally stressed over the fact that they dropped the ball or the fact that a referee made a few poor calls. They become convinced that because it happened once, it will happen again. Worrying over things that happened in the past prevents a person from enjoying the present—and if you're not enjoying the present moment of sports, you're more likely to exhibit poor sportsmanship.

Although many people find watching golf terribly boring, I like to watch it because I like how someone like Tiger Woods or David Duvall is able to follow up a really horrible shot with a perfect little chip shot onto the green. They really exemplify how athletes can put the past behind them (even if it was a past that only happened a minute or two ago) and concentrate on the next shot. If you are having a problem with a child who continually dwells on his or her past mistakes, you might try having him or her watch a golf match with you. Point out how even the best golfers make bad shots, and how they frequently follow up those bad shots with really good shots. Discuss what would happen if Tiger Woods (or some other golfer you are watching) were to let himself stay discouraged over a bad shot. Ask your child what he or she thinks golfers do in order to put a bad shot behind them and move on. Ask how your child could incorporate these actions into his or her own life. (For further ideas, see the section on "Letting It Go" in Chapter 2, "A Good Sport Knows How to Lose.")

• **Confidence buster: focusing on the negative.** Have you ever known a child like this? The child receives A's in almost all of his or her classes, but the only grade he or she notices is that one B+. Or, the child hits the ball every time he or she steps up to the plate except once, and that one miss is the only thing you hear about all the way home. People who exhibit this kind of negativity— whether they are athletes, coaches, or parents—make it hard for anyone else to enjoy the experience. They're like little clouds raining on everyone's parade.

Sometimes you get a child who focuses on the negative because he or she is one of those perfectionists we talked about earlier. But not everyone who focuses on the negative is a perfectionist. Some people do it as a protective tool. For instance, if every time your child starts talking to you about the good game he or she had, your first response is to say, "Yeah, but you know, you really gotta work more on your defense; I saw your man getting past you a lot out there," then pretty soon your child is going to learn to head you off at the pass by focusing on the negative before you do. If the child can say it first, then he or she won't experience the hurt of having you say it.

To help break your child of the habit of focusing on the negative, first make sure that you aren't part of the problem. Then explain to your child that we all have an inner voice that we use to talk to ourselves; if all we're hearing from that inner voice is negative stuff, then we're going to perform poorly. Help the child learn how to retrain his or her inner voice to say positive things.

This is called "positive self-talk." One trick that I used to help quell my negative inner voice was to write positive statements on a stack of index cards and carry those around with me. When I had a few spare moments, I would read through those statements, and they would help me keep positive thoughts in my head.

Being Secure in Who You Are

There once was a college basketball player who was accused of being "too nice." His response was, "I don't have to talk trash. I let my game speak for itself."

Confident athletes don't need to trash talk or display other traits of poor sportsmanship just to make themselves "look good." They have an inner confidence—a sense of personal well-being—that allows them to follow the beat of their own drummer. This inner confidence is not tied to their status on the team or how many wins they have or anything like that. It is tied to their own knowledge that they have prepared to the best of their ability and will do the best job they can.

There is a difference between being confident and having a big head. A big head is what athletes have when they pull the "Do you know who I am?" line on people. A big head is what athletes have when they get upset that other athletes, coaches, teammates, or others aren't showing them the respect that they think they deserve.

David Robinson of the San Antonio Spurs has the kind of inner confidence (not "big head" confidence) that all athletes should aspire to. As a naval officer, an accomplished pianist, a strong family man, and a compassionate community member, Robinson is secure enough in his own person to not have to descend to the unsportsmanlike level of some of his fellow NBA players. Robinson and "nice-guy" teammate Tim Duncan were often accused of not having what it took to take their team to the top, until in 1999 the Spurs proved that nice guys *can* finish first.

This kind of inner confidence doesn't come solely from having well-developed sports skills. To the contrary, athletes who focus primarily on developing their sports skills often lack this crucial kind of confidence. I know, because I was one of them. From the time I was eight until my early twenties, my life revolved completely around sports. On the court, I felt confident in my ability to perform. Off the court, I felt just the opposite. Other than being an athlete, I had no idea who I was or what I wanted to do with my life.

The best way to help young athletes develop a sense of security in who they are is to make sure they are well-rounded individuals. It can be tempting, especially when an athlete shows exceptional talent, to focus on that talent to the exclusion of everything else. *Parents should avoid doing this at all cost.* Richard Williams, who decided early on that he was going to raise his daughters, Venus and Serena, to be tennis champions, also decided that he was going to work just as hard to ensure that they grew up to be educated young women who knew how to take care of themselves in a variety of situations. I think a large part of the Williams sisters' confidence on the court can be attributed to their many talents and interests off the court.

How do you help your children achieve the kind of well-balanced life that contributes to their sense of confidence? You begin by exposing them to a variety of experiences. Besides taking them to sporting events, you can also take them to concerts, museums, historical landmarks, and so on. You encourage their non-sports interests. You encourage their coaches to encourage their non-sports interests. I know that many coaches would prefer their athletes to focus on just one sport, or on sports, period. If any of your children run into this kind of coach, you may have to help them learn how to negotiate with the coach so that they have the opportunity to explore a variety of interests—such as participating in sports and being in the school play at the same time.[6]

One thing you do need to watch out for is the child who tries to do *too* much, because this can lead to burnout and failure. Instead of building confidence, kids who try to do too much can find their confidence destroyed.

While I was watching my grandson's tennis lesson one day, I was approached by a parent who was concerned about his fifteen-year-old son. The boy played tennis and basketball, worked on the school newspaper, played a musical instrument, and got mostly A's in school. "I think it's too much for him, but he seems to enjoy all these activities and doesn't want to give anything up," the dad said. "What should I do?"

My response was that the dad shouldn't push his son to give up any of these activities. He should, however, communicate the message that while he admires and appreciates all his son is doing, his love and appreciation will be just as great if his son chooses to scale back on one or more of his interests. As a parent, your job is to assess whether the situation is healthy or not and only step in if you sense that your child's well-being is at stake. As long as your child is learning and having fun, then I wouldn't worry. But if children start taking themselves and their activities too seriously, then I would say they have a problem that needs to be dealt with.

What are some of the other confidence busters that parents need to watch out for?

• **Confidence buster: wanting everybody's approval.** This is an unattainable and unrealistic goal. It is better for young people to develop personal standards and values that are not completely dependent on the approval of others. For instance, when I watch Christian at his ball games and his tennis practices, I notice that if his dad is there, Christian's eyes are constantly darting over to him, seeking his approval. Interestingly, he doesn't do that with me—probably because he knows that he is number one with me regardless of his performance.

Once again, this relates to confidence as an inner thing. We need to continually emphasize to our children that what other people think of them shouldn't matter as much as what they think of themselves.

• **Confidence buster: putting too much emphasis on what you "should" do.** "Should" statements are often perfectionistic and reflect others' expectations rather than what the athlete wants and desires. Anytime you hear your children talking about "I should" or "I ought to," this is a red flag. "Shoulds" and "ought tos" refer to the ideal—the way things would be in a perfect world. Instead, teach your children to use phrases like "I want to" and "I choose to." If they can't say these phrases (and mean them), then maybe they need to reevaluate whether they are really doing what they want to be doing.

Self-Confidence Breeds Courage

The ultimate measure of a man is not where he stands at times of comfort and convenience but where he stands at times of challenge.
—Martin Luther King[7]

Courage is misunderstood in our society. Too often, we think of courage as being the ability to act without fear. In reality, courage is the ability to act in spite of fear.

As your children strive to model the sportsmanship actions discussed in this book, there will be times when people will make fun of them. There will be times when people will try to intimidate them. There will be times when people will try to exclude them. That is why you need to help them develop a sure foundation of self-confidence and belief in themselves. This foundation will better enable them to be true to their convictions even when those convictions are unpopular or inconvenient.

In her book *Raising Winners*, Shari Young Kuchenbecker shares the story of a young man who, as a freshman on the baseball team, found himself the target of hazing by the older players. After the first day of what was supposed to be a weeklong indoctrination, the boy was quiet and withdrawn at dinner that night. His parents finally got him to open up about what had happened and how he felt about it. The boy decided that it was a stupid tradition and he didn't like it. With his parents' encouragement, he thought of what he could say to the team captain the next day, and then he called the other two freshman players and got them to agree to meet with him, the team captain, and the coach. The hazing was immediately discontinued. And when the boy became a senior, he was elected team captain—because his teammates knew they could depend on him as a leader.[8]

Children learn *about* courage through stories, games, role-playing, and discussions with parents or others. But children learn to *have* courage through their own experiences. As a parent, you need to be careful that you don't step in too quickly to solve your child's problems or to try and make things easier for him or her. But you also don't want to be like the father who taught his son to swim by throwing him in the lake! Instead, encourage your children to take acceptable risks, such as trying out for an unfamiliar sport, or for the school play. Know when to let your children stand up for themselves (at the same time, help them learn the skills they need to stand up for themselves by role-playing different situations with them). Let your children see you taking risks and learning from your mistakes.

When you encourage your children's moves toward self-reliance and accept and love them no matter what, your children learn to accept themselves and develop the kind of self-confidence that will make sport a more enjoyable and meaningful experience for themselves and for those around them.

MODEL-TEACH-ENCOURAGE

1. As much as possible, let your children make their own sports decisions.
2. Encourage your children to be self-sufficient. This could include having them pack their own snacks for practice, take care of their own equipment, wash their uniforms, etc.
3. Help your children improve their sports competency. Spend time practicing with them, or have an older, more skilled child offer them some pointers.
4. Support your children whether they make the team or not. (Remember, Michael Jordan didn't make his high school varsity basketball team until his junior year.)
5. Examine your own expectations. Are you expecting too much from your children? Are you pushing them too hard to excel in sports?
6. Express confidence in your children. Give them lots of positive (but honest) feedback.
7. Teach your children how to visualize. Show them how to "see" themselves performing successfully in different situations.
8. Take steps to ensure that your children's sports experiences are inclusive. When athletes of different skill levels and backgrounds are made to feel welcome and a part of the team, it helps boost everyone's confidence and self-esteem.

9. Help your children have realistic expectations regarding their own developmental process. Encourage them to focus on their own improvement, not on how they compare to friends, family members, or teammates.
10. Never compare your children to others.
11. Help your children to set their own standards. Discourage them from being too dependent on the approval of others.
12. Children usually want to be good at something right away, and become frustrated when they aren't. Explain to your children that if they want to improve, they will have to work at it. Anything worth getting is worth working for.
13. If your children have a problem in sports, ask them what they think they should do to fix it. Encourage them to take action for themselves.
14. Monitor your children's coaches to make sure they use positive language when speaking to your children. A coach who uses insults or frequently criticizes athletes is doing psychological harm.
15. Encourage your children to look for opportunities to increase their teammates' self-confidence. Do not allow them to insult or criticize their teammates.
16. Encourage your children to have a variety of friends. Often, athletes (especially elite athletes) hang out primarily with other athletes, which can lead them to feel self-conscious or not as confident around nonathletes.
17. Emphasize your children's strengths. Focus on what they *can* do (catch the ball, show good sportsmanship), not on what they *can't* do (throw an accurate pass, see the open player).
18. Encourage your children to take risks by looking at new experiences as opportunities to learn rather than occasions to win or lose.

19. Teach your children how to use positive self-talk. Show them how to catch themselves making harmful assumptions. Then, show them how to stop and substitute more reasonable assumptions.
20. Give your child opportunities to try out many new experiences.
21. Foster responsible behavior in your children by giving them meaningful chores to be responsible for.
22. Give your children positive encouragement to keep practicing the things they like or seem to be good at. Try to stress the joy in mastering a skill, rather than suggesting that mastery will make your children "better."

A Good Sport Gives Back

Why not use the name recognition to bring about positive change?
. . . Players of responsibility can do great work.
—STEVE YOUNG, FORMER SAN FRANCISCO 49ERS QUARTERBACK[1]

The actions that we've talked about up to this point—knowing how to lose, understanding the difference between winning and success, respecting others—are, for the most part, things that are reasonable to associate with athletes and sportsmanship. But "giving back"? Taking yourself out of the spotlight so another player can shine, or working on community service projects—isn't this a little above and beyond the call of duty as good sports?

Yes, it is. And that is why giving back is an essential part of our new definition of sportsmanship. It is part of raising the bar. It is part of creating athletes who don't just care about sports, but who care about their sports communities. It is part of creating a community of good sports—communities of parents, athletes, and coaches working together to empower children, strengthen families, and unite individuals.

Why is giving back important? To begin with, giving back connects us to each other. When you teach your children to give back, you're teaching them how to reach out to other people. Sometimes the person they're reaching out to may be a teammate. It may be someone in your family. It may be someone your child has never met before and will never meet again. No matter who it is, establishing a connection with others involves getting to know them as individuals. Sports can provide children with opportunities to do this that they might not normally have.

For example, in 1994, the Redlands (California) High School football team began its "Dream Team" program, where students from the school's special education department serve as team managers. Not only does this program give the special education students a chance to participate, but it also gives the football players the chance to be in touch with a segment of society they might not otherwise come in contact with. Football players note that the program has had a positive effect on how they interact with developmentally disabled classmates. As the mother of one "Dream Team" member said of the football players, "They'll take that with them after high school and be sensitive, caring people all through their lives because they weren't separated according to ability levels."[2]

Giving back is also important because it helps you teach your children empathy. Empathy is the ability to detect, understand, and appropriately respond to the perspective and feelings of others. In a sense, it is the ability to feel what others are feeling.

Not long ago, I read about a touching display of empathy on the part of a young basketball player. The day after high school freshman Candace Wiggins won a state sportsmanship award for leading her team to California's Division V title, she and her teammates were saddened to learn that the young man who portrayed the school's unofficial mascot had been killed in a car accident. At the boy's memorial service, Wiggins gave her sportsmanship and state championship medals to the boy's mother, JoAnne. "I just wanted to show JoAnne that Kenner was more important to us than the state championship," Wiggins said.[3]

As parents, we are very familiar with empathy. When our kindergartner comes home from school crying because the other kids were teasing her, we remember what it was like to be teased, and we feel her pain. It hurts us every bit as much as it does her.

However, empathy can be a challenging thing to teach to children because of their natural tendency toward self-centeredness. I have found that one of the best ways to encourage empathy in my grandchildren is to nudge them with questions such as, "How do you think that person felt when that happened?" or, "If you do that to this person, what do you think he will feel like?"

I also try to get my grandchildren to think of other people's needs. For instance, "Christian, Grandma has been having a very bad day today. She doesn't feel well, and the lady at the department store spoke very sharply to her. What do you think Grandma needs from us today to help make her day better?"

Research has shown that children who learn empathy are less likely to have behavioral problems and are more likely to be socially competent. Empathy is also a factor in the control of aggressive behavior. Without empathy, the aggressiveness that is a natural part of sports competition could easily turn into savagery. Because empathy enables children and adolescents to consider multiple points of view, they are less likely to misinterpret events and intentions. For example, an athlete who is able to empathize with his or her opponents would be more likely to shrug off trash talk or a hard hit as frustration or desperation. A less empathetic player would be more inclined to retaliate, thus escalating the level of unsportsmanlike conduct.

I don't think there's ever been a greater need than right now for individuals who can empathize with others. If Osama bin Laden and his followers had had one shred of empathy for their victims they never could have committed the atrocities that they did. If we are to prevent similar atrocities from happening, then we need to raise children who are able to reach out to others with empathy and understanding—both on the sports field and off.

Another reason that giving back is important is that it helps to strengthen the institution of sports. Leah O'Brien-Amico, starting right fielder for the two-time Olympic gold medal–winning women's softball team, has spent a lot of her spare time working with the Murrieta (California) Valley Girls Softball Association. "We have only a couple days off and if I can talk with the kids and help them out in any way, then I would choose to spend my time that way," she said. "It is so important now that these kids are able to have role models. . . . When I was growing up, I didn't have a lot of role models to look up to. . . . The sport has done a lot for me in my life and I want it to do the same for others."[4]

Where would youth sports be without all the many individuals who volunteer their time and talents as coaches, umpires, ticket takers, chauffeurs, team parents, etc.? Where would it be without those individuals who donate money to build fields, buy uniforms, provide treats, and so on?

When you encourage your children to give back to sports—to serve as volunteer coaches and officials, to help others the same way they were helped—you are establishing a habit of giving that will not only stay with them throughout their lives, but will help them to create the kind of "good sports" communities that we talked of earlier.

Finally, giving back is important because it helps fill our deep human need to have purposeful lives. In his classic book *Man's Search for Meaning*, Dr. Viktor Frankl talked about his experience as a prisoner in Nazi concentration camps during World War II. As Frankl watched himself and his comrades being stripped of everything—families, possessions, health, dignity—he wondered why some prisoners were able to survive and even rise above the suffering, while others had a completely different reaction. He finally determined that the ones that were able to survive the starvation and torture were the ones who had a purpose to their lives—such as something they felt they needed to do or a loved one they wanted to see. Without this sense of purpose people gave up and died, or succumbed to the baser side of human nature.

I think this is one reason why, at age sixty-seven, I am putting so much time and effort into my nonprofit work for Parents for Good Sports. Numerous health issues have led me to believe that Willard Scott probably won't be wishing me a "Happy One-Hundredth Birthday!" from the "Today" show. Thus I find it extremely important at this stage in my life to feel that what I am doing has purpose and meaning beyond that of merely providing for my family's material needs. Because sport has played such a predominant part in my life, it is to sport that I want to give back. It has become my life's purpose.

"Giving Back" on the Field

When I first mentioned giving back, the first thing that probably popped into your mind was community service of some kind. That is certainly one way an athlete can give back, and we will discuss that shortly. But there are ways that athletes can demonstrate "giving back" *on* the field, as well. For instance, just being a role model—in the way they play and the way they act—is one way that athletes can give back.

I was impressed by the story I read about a UCLA basketball player who, as a freshman, had found himself virtually ignored by the senior players. He decided when he was a senior he was going to make a point to help out the younger guys. As a fifth-year senior, he stuck to that promise—even to the point of forgoing his relatively spacious (and quiet) off-campus apartment to share a dorm room with a bunch of noisy freshmen. There, he can effectively model the kind of commitment to sports and academics that young people are so desperately in need of.

How can you help your children to be role models for those around them? One way is to encourage them to use their talents (athletic and otherwise) to support school and community activities. In one small rural town, members of the football team sprint from football practice to play rehearsal, knowing that if they don't participate in drama, there won't be enough bodies to put on a play. Not all of the players are dramatically inclined, but they all feel a responsibility to support their classmates' interests in the same way that their classmates support them.

You could also have a family activity where all of you talk about your favorite sports figures. The qualification: the person has to be someone who has given back to his or her community in some way. You can talk about how these individuals have influenced you, and then discuss how the members of your family could in turn influence others.

Athletes also have the opportunity to give back on the field in their interactions with their teammates. We talked about teamwork in depth in Chapter Five, so we don't need to go into it too extensively here. However, I do think that one way you can encourage your children to be better team players is to remind them that it is part of giving back.

Again, it can be challenging—but rewarding—to get your children to exhibit this kind of unselfishness. In *The 7 Habits of Highly Effective Families*, Stephen Covey shares the story of a young girl who at first had no desire to give back to a difficult teammate. The two girls had been good friends until the first girl started playing quite well and getting quite a bit of attention. Jealous, the teammate (Pam) stopped passing the ball. In frustration, the girl turned to her father for advice:

> After a long discussion, my dad told me that the best thing he could think of was to give Pam the ball every time I got it. Every time. I thought it was the stupidest suggestion he had ever given me. He told me it would work and left me at the kitchen table to think about it. But I didn't. I knew it wouldn't work and put it aside as silly fatherly advice.

For the next game I planned and plotted and went out with a mission to ruin Pam's game. On my first possession of the ball, I heard my dad above the crowd. He had a booming voice, and though I shut out everything around me while playing basketball, I could always hear Dad's deep voice. At the moment I caught the ball, he yelled out, "Give her the ball!" I hesitated for one second then did what I knew was right. Although I was open for a shot, I found Pam and passed her the ball. She was shocked for a moment, then turned and shot, sinking the ball for two points.

As I ran down the court to play defense, I felt something I had never felt before: true joy for the success of another human being. And, even more, I realized that it put us ahead in the game. It felt good to be winning. I continued to give her the ball every time I got it in the first half. Every time. In the second half I did the same, shooting only if it was a designated play or if I was wide open for a shot.

We won that game, and in the games that followed, Pam began to pass me the ball as much as I passed it to her. Our teamwork was getting stronger and stronger, and so was our friendship. We won the majority of our games that year and became a legendary small town duo. The local newspaper even did an article on our ability to pass to each other and sense each other's presence. It was as if we could read each other's mind. Overall, I scored more points than ever before. When I scored, I could feel her genuine happiness for me. And when she scored more than I did, I felt especially good inside.[5]

"Giving back" to one's teammates doesn't always involve giving up the ball. One high school quarterback went so far as to give up his entire identity. His friend, Mitch Duckworth (the team's wide receiver), was seriously ill and couldn't play in the state championship game. Unbeknownst to the fans, parents, referees, and the sportswriters covering the game, the young quarterback slipped his sick friend's jersey over his head, and wore it for the entire game.

The next morning's newspaper read "Brighton managed three quick-strike touchdowns in the second half, and 52 of those yards came on Mitch Duckworth's pass to Cowan late in the second quarter." "Duckworth led the Bengals with 80 rushing yards, including a 3-yard TD run and a 49-yard TD pass to Donnie Saba."[6] In this day and age of headline-grabbing sports stars, it's nice to know that at least one athlete cared less about seeing his name in the paper than he did about wanting to help a friend.

As you share stories like this with your children, ask them to reflect on how these stories make them feel. Ask them if they would like to be on a team where people work together and look out for each other like the individuals in the stories. What are some things they could do to make their teams like that?

From giving back to one's teammates (whom one supposedly knows and cares about), it is only a short step to teaching your children how to give back to people who aren't on their team, or whom they might not know well or know at all. In other words, it is time to teach them not just how to be good citizens of their sports communities, but how they can use sport to become good citizens of their global community.

"Giving Back" off the Field

Ashe always embodied good sportsmanship on the playing field. But if sportsmanship is also an athlete's ability to shift from being a selfish competitor to being a useful member of society, then Ashe's sportsmanship is unequaled. His gradual harvest has grown into a mountain of good.

—SPORTS ILLUSTRATED, DECEMBER 1992[7]

Ultimately, what do you want sport to do for your children? You want it to make them better people. For most parents, this translates to kids who know how to take risks, overcome challenges, be good losers (and winners), learn new skills, and work together as a team.

Those are good things. But sport has the potential to do much more than that for our children. In the hands of the right people, sport has the potential to change the world.

At the very least, sport has the potential to change Colton, California.

It is in Colton that Coach Harold Strauss has made community service as much a part of football as, well, the football. Players do everything from participating in town parades to cleaning up dilapidated homes for elderly women. They also serve as coaches for a summer youth camp.

The Colton High football players are lucky to have a coach who puts as big a priority on giving back as he does on giving hits. Not all athletes will be as fortunate. That's why it is up to parents to take the lead in teaching children how to give back.

As a nation, we witnessed no greater examples of "giving back" than those that occurred in relation to the September 11 tragedy. From the firemen and policemen who selflessly gave their lives to save others, to those civilians who fought and triumphed over the terrorists on Flight 93, ordinary individuals acted in extraordinary ways.

According to Samuel Oliner, coauthor of *The Altruistic Personality*, an individual's family background plays a large part in whether he or she will grow up to be the type of person who is able to give back so unselfishly. People who "give back" tend to:

- Have parents who reason with them and explain how their actions might hurt others
- Have parents who volunteer in the community
- Be exposed to more diverse people in their homes

- Have affectionate homes and good role models
- Have families who participate in activities together and spend a lot of time talking to each other[8]

What are some other things you can do with your children to raise them with the desire to give back to others? I know families who have created family "mission statements," which describe how they see themselves as a family and what things are important to them. Perhaps you could create a family "sports mission statement." As a family, talk about how you want your family to be when it comes to sports. (For example, "We are a family that sees sport as a way to strengthen ourselves, our family, and our community.") Include the values that are important to you, along with ways you feel your family can contribute to your sports community.

Another thing you can do is family volunteer work. Sometimes parents hesitate to involve their children in community service (especially when kids are young) because they think, "Oh, the kids will be bored," or, "They won't really understand what we're doing." But I know that families who do this say their most meaningful memories have come through these shared experiences.

Also, don't take for granted that just because your kid is a "good kid," that he or she is always going to do the right thing. Even with the best of kids, it sometimes takes parental nudging to get them to step outside their sometimes limited sports perspective. Michelle Kwan, known as a very down-to-earth and giving athlete, has occasionally had to be reminded by her parents to not use her stardom as an excuse for putting herself first.

> When a tired Michelle took a back exit at a tour stop last year to avoid signing autographs, [her father] Danny got her off the bus and told her those fans spent a lot of time and money to see her, and she had an obligation to spend a few minutes with them.
>
> When Kwan failed her driver's test last fall on a three-point turn, Danny asked his daughter to write the instructor a thank-

you note for reminding her how important safety is. She answers every fan letter and sends Christmas cards to sportswriters. Kwan donates to sick children the hundreds of stuffed animals that fans throw on the ice.[9]

Your children don't have to be professional athletes to make a big impact on their community. Marcus Houston was one of the top prep recruits in the nation in 1999. Throughout his school career, Houston used his athletic skills as a springboard for helping others. "I'm in a spotlight position," Houston said. "If I can make things better, I need to take advantage of that."

All of the Houston kids became athletes, but their parents encouraged them to do more. For instance, they were all expected to run for office. "It made them aware of their school and the needs of their schoolmates," their father said. "They didn't have to win, but they had to develop a platform."

As a family, the Houstons also participated in community service projects. Whenever something was happening in the community, you could count on seeing the Houstons there.

The Houstons like to say that sport does not define them, it complements them. Maybe this explains what happened when Marcus, after becoming a star at Thomas Jefferson High, noticed his teammates failing classes.

"You can talk about the epidemic failure of inner-city schools," he says. "But unless you're doing something about it, you can't point any fingers."

Sports was a vehicle for change. Marcus knew that younger students looked up to him because he was an All-City player. He designed a presentation called "Just Say Know."

Visiting middle schools throughout the Denver area, he showed a brief highlight film of his games—"to captivate their attention," he says—then spoke at length about the importance of school.

Students were encouraged to enter his contest, writing about what success meant to them and how they might achieve it. The winner received $50, a pizza party, and a limousine ride to a Thomas Jefferson game.

Marcus paid for the prizes with money he earned mowing lawns and shoveling snow.

"When you hear these things about him, you think, golly, nobody can be that good," says Len Ashford, an assistant principal at Thomas Jefferson. "I've been in education 32 years and I've never met someone who matches these qualities."

. . . His efforts [in filing a civil rights lawsuit after police allegedly used racial epithets and excessive force in breaking up a fistfight that broke out during a dance at Thomas Jefferson] attracted the attention of Amnesty International, which invited Marcus to Amsterdam to speak at a conference. He was 17 years old and only a junior. Again, he would have to sacrifice.

The conference took place at the same time his team was playing for the city championship.

"That was a tough choice," he says. "But in the long term, the impact of speaking about human rights was more than the impact of playing in a football game."

. . . Every time he wins an award, he also thinks about how he can use it to get more funds for "Just Say Know." Every time he gets attention for his exploits on the field, he reminds himself that football is only one piece of life's puzzle.[10]

Because this kind of altruism doesn't come naturally to most human beings (especially most *young* human beings), it is crucial for adults to set the example. Marcus Houston's parents set an example. Michelle Kwan's parents set an example. Coach Harold Strauss set an example.

For many years now, I have participated in the annual Volleyball Festival held in Sacramento, California. The Volleyball Festival draws thousands of young women from across the country to compete against and learn from one another. At the completion of the 2001 Festival, I received the following letter:

I am the father of a 12-year-old participating in our first (of what I hope will be many) Festivals. It's quite an event; the founders and sponsors should be very proud of this accomplishment.

The true purpose of this post is not so much to sincerely thank you for giving my daughter the opportunity to play on a national level, but to pass along to the committee an event of sportsmanship the likes of which I have not witnessed in my 30 years of competing and coaching competitive athletics.

The Bakersfield Select 12's came into the Davis Festival ranked sixth. Quite a lofty seed, but if they played their best, a ranking justified nonetheless. On Monday night, after winning their first two matches, the Bakersfield squad faced West Slope (seeded 44th). As you might expect, the match was rather one-sided, although the West Slope gals fought valiantly. One particular young lady on the West Slope team came to serve. She tossed the ball into the air twice, yet did not swing. On the third attempt, she made a cross-armed move, but the ball fell well short of the net. Her second service turn had the same result and as the match continued, it was evident to me sitting in the stands that she was at a low ebb.

The match concluded [and] Bakersfield was very gracious, but what happened next brought me to tears. The Bakersfield coach, already the recipient of four strings of beads on the first day [Festival participants were awarded "beads" for exhibiting sportsmanship and spirit], walked across the court seeking out the little girl as she was sitting in the stands despondent over her play. Kneeling over the little girl, the coach spoke something in the girl's ear. She then proceeded to take a string of beads from her neck and place them around the girl. The child's reaction was immediate, the smile was indescribable.

I don't know how many people saw this act of kindness, or sportsmanship if you like, but I did and it will be with me the rest of my life.

Summer Sanders has said that when it came to her brother's and her sports participation, her parents were always an example to her because of their focus on sport as a character-forming experience. "For our parents, the Olympics were just another leg in our journey; the Games were never a destination beyond which nothing mattered. What was important to them was how we played the game, not whether or not we won. What was important was that we were givers, not takers—that we gave our best in whatever we did, and that ultimately we gave of ourselves in such a way that we left the world a better place than we found it."[11]

Near the end of Arthur Ashe's life, after he had been diagnosed with AIDS received from a blood transfusion, a reporter asked the former tennis great why he continued to work so hard on his social programs. Why didn't he just take it easy—spend the remainder of his days playing with his daughter or being with his wife? Ashe's answer was that you play out your match, you pound away as hard as you can at what you care about until your life is over, for the perfectly practical reason that we are not here in a vacuum.[12]

Arthur Ashe never felt like just being an athlete was enough. He felt that, as an athlete—especially as a famous athlete—he had a responsibility to use his money and talents and name recognition to help others. That, for him, was true "winning."

At the end of your child's sports experience, can you say that you have used sport to help your child become a giver, not a taker?

Have you used it to help your child become a better person? To help your child make a better world?

If so, then you can truly say that your child's sports experience has been a successful one. You can truly say that you have raised a *good* sport.

Congratulations!

MODEL—TEACH—ENCOURAGE

1. Discuss with your children the importance of "giving back." Ask them for their ideas on how each one of you can give back to other members of your family, people in your neighborhood, people at school, teammates, and other members of the sports community and the community at large.
2. Involve your whole family in community service.
3. Consider creating a family sports mission statement. Write this mission statement down and hang it in a prominent place in your home.
4. Discuss with your children the importance of caring more about the quality of the overall sports experience (in other words, the well-being of everyone involved) than about who wins or loses.
5. Help your children set goals other than winning. It's okay for winning to be a goal, but they should also have goals such as having fun, working as a team, etc. That way, they can say that they may not have achieved the goal of winning, but they achieved their other goals. This helps to create a win/win spirit.
6. Encourage your children to give back to one another by teaching each other sports skills or other skills.

7. Ask your children what thing they might do to better understand each other and other people. Help them think of concrete things to do (such as not interrupting when people are speaking, listening without trying to think of their response, not replying immediately but taking time to think about what the person has said, etc.). Role-play good listening habits.

8. To better understand how to model empathy and understanding with your children, read *The 7 Habits of Highly Effective Families*, "Habit 5: Seek First to Understand . . . Then to Be Understood."

9. Help your children understand and appreciate others' differences by exposing them to different cultures, perspectives, etc.

10. Show your children how much fun it is to give back. Do "Secret Pals" within your family or as a family. For instance, as a family you could choose different members of your child's team to do secret kindnesses for.

11. Share a story of how an instance of giving back (either to the community or to an individual) has touched you.

EPILOGUE

Because Sportsmanship Matters

Sports is not an end but a means. It can become a vehicle of civility and genuine fun, pushing people to give the best of themselves on the field, shunning that which can be of danger or serious damage to themselves or others.

—POPE JOHN PAUL II[1]

I do believe we don't need one more negative influence in a world that already has too many.

—AL MARTINEZ, COLUMNIST, *LOS ANGELES TIMES*[2]

When the players took the floor in Washington during the 2001 NBA All-Star Weekend rookie-sophomore game, Andre Miller was ready. Miller, playing for the second-year pros, remembered only too well the boos he'd received the previous year for choosing to make a simple layup over a flashy dunk.

"If I've got the energy, I'm going to go up and dunk," Miller said. "Obviously I learned my lesson from last year."

What lesson did he learn? That sportsmanship is less valued than showmanship? That the end justifies the means? That glory beats honor any day?

I know one lesson he didn't learn—at least, not from the crowd that booed him. The lesson? That sportsmanship matters.

Why does sportsmanship matter? It matters for all the reasons we have talked about in this book—because it keeps kids safe, it teaches them valuable lessons, and it makes sport more fun. But more than anything else, sportsmanship matters because it is part of what constitutes being a good citizen. When we create good sports, we are creating good people.

The implications of this reverberate far beyond the athletic field. Because sportsmanship develops the character of the participants, it contributes to the strength and civility of sports and ultimately, society. Has there ever been a greater need for young people who know the difference between what is right and what is wrong and who are willing to practice sportsmanship every single day in their homes, their schools, and their communities?

Sportsmanship matters because your children's success, happiness, and well-being depend in large part on who they are inside, not on what they have or how they look. Sportsmanship is about who you are on the inside. Lessons about healthy competition and sportsmanship learned in youth can influence how your children live out their personal and professional lives. It can influence whether your children turn out to be mothers and fathers, employees and citizens, who are interested primarily in being number one and getting "what's theirs," or whether they place more importance on seeking the common good.

Sportsmanship matters because without it, how can you really enjoy the journey that is sport? My daughter is a physician. She sees this problem daily in her patients' lives, as well as in her own—the need to take the time to enjoy the journey of life. Without sportsmanship, goodwill, or caring for others, the journey of sport loses a great deal of its joy and meaning.

Other than religion, I can think of nothing that works as well as sport to bring out the best in us. However, just as religion has had its Inquisitions, its Holy Wars, and its September 11s, so has sport had its rioting fans, its murderous parents, and its XFL.

In the Introduction to this book I wrote:

As stories of athletes raising money for victims of September's tragedy replaced stories of athletes just plain raising hell, I was not naive enough to think that this "kinder, gentler" version of sport was here to stay. The further removed we became from September 11, the more likely it was that we *would* return to normal. And in the case of sport, that was not necessarily a good thing.

It took all of three months for sport to get back to normal. During the first week of December, while the families of those who died on September 11 were contemplating the loneliness of a holiday season spent without loved ones, the fans of the Cleveland Browns were contemplating the best way to make complete idiots of themselves. They decided they would do it by staging a mini-riot over a fourth-down catch that was ruled incomplete, thus showing how much they "cared" about their team. As bottles and other objects rained down on the field, one fan said he would never forget the look of terror on the face of a three-year-old boy whose grandmother had brought him to his first Browns game.[3]

These are not the memories we want our children to have of sport. These are not the lessons we want our children to learn. These are not the lessons of sportsmanship.

It is my hope that this book will help parents work together with their children to create a new breed of sportsmen and sportswomen—one that recognizes that for sport to achieve its full potential in their lives and the lives of others, it must be built upon the cornerstones of good sports: respect, civility, responsibility, and community.

Sport has often been tied to people's desire to compete, to outdo, to dominate, and even to go to war. Yet, as I have set out to prove here, sport can just as easily be the medium that shows kids how to cooperate, help others, search for harmony, and end conflict.

Can't you just picture it? Can't you just picture a world of individuals who are willing to look beyond racial, cultural, and religious differences to seek mutually beneficial solutions to problems—and all because they learned how to do it as kids on the playing field?

When you get right down to it, any time you are talking about sports—above points scored, championships won, and trophies hoisted—there should only be one thing that truly matters.

Sportsmanship.

ENDNOTES

Introduction

1. Alison Jones, ed., *Chambers Dictionary of Quotations*, Chambers, New York, 1997, 745.
2. S. K. Stoll, *Sportsmanship: Dead or Alive?* (unpublished manuscript, University of Idaho, Center for Ethical Theory and Honor in Competitive Sports, 1992).
3. J. M. Beller and S. K. Stoll, *Division I Athletes: Sportsmanship Qualities* (unpublished manuscript, University of Idaho, Center for Ethical Theory and Honor in Competitive Sports, 1992).
4. Ibid.
5. J. M. Beller, *Quantitative and Qualitative Measures of Moral Reasoning and Development of High School Teacher/Coaches* (unpublished manuscript, Eastern Michigan University, 1992).
6. Craig Clifford and Randolph Feezell, *Coaching for Character: Reclaiming the Principles of Sportsmanship* (Champaign, IL: Human Kinetics, 1997), 12.
7. Russell Gough, *Character Is Everything: Promoting Ethical Excellence in Sports* (Fort Worth, TX: Harcourt Brace, 1997), 21.
8. *Olympism: Lighting the Way to a Legacy of Peace* (Griffin Publishing/United States Olympic Committee, 1996), ix.
9. Ibid.

Chapter 1

1. Angela Lumpkin, Sharon Kay Stoll, and Jennifer M. Beller, *Sports Ethics: Applications for Fair Play*, 2d ed. (New York: McGraw-Hill, 1999), 4.
2. Ibid., 11.
3. Stephen Covey, *Principle-Centered Leadership* (New York: Summit, 1991), 18–19.
4. Elizabeth Pantley, *Kid Cooperation* (Oakland, CA: New Harbinger, 1996), 119.

Chapter 2

1. Summer Sanders, *Champions Are Raised, Not Born* (New York: Delacorte, 1999), 135.
2. Rob Gilbert, ed., *Bits and Pieces*, vol. T, no. 23.
3. Sanders, 199.
4. Quoted in Jane Clifford, "Fatal Scuffle Between Dads a Deadly Lesson," *San Diego Union-Tribune*, July 15, 2000.
5. Karen S. Peterson, "Why Everyone Is So Short-Tempered," *USA Today*, July 18, 2000.
6. Erica Thesing, "Youth Sports World Is a Rage," *Sacramento Bee*, July 13, 2000.
7. Bill Plaschke, "One-Punch Knockout," *Los Angeles Times*, May 28, 2000.
8. Doug Smith, " 'Genius with Racket' Changed Tennis' Attitudes," *USA Today*, July 8, 1999.
9. Doug Robinson, "Wildcat Player Shocked at His Loss of Control," *Deseret News*, December 1, 1998.
10. Diana Griego Erwin, "Ice Rink Killing No Blot on Kid Sports," *Sacramento Bee*, July 13, 2000.

11. Cornelia Maude Spelman, *When I Feel Angry* (Morton Grove, IL: Albert Whitman, 2000, from the "Note to Parents").
12. Bill Bradley, "Whatever the Score—Bounce Back," *Parade Magazine*, October 18, 1998, 4.
13. Sanders, 93.
14. Ibid., 137–8, 142.
15. Marilyn Elias, "Widow of Sept. 11 Hero Carries On," *USA Today*, November 21, 2001.
16. William Pollack, *Real Boys: Rescuing Our Sons from the Myths of Boyhood* (New York: Random House, 1998), 281.
17. "Whatever the Score—Bounce Back," *Parade Magazine*, October 18, 1998.
18. Steve Spring, "Rahman Has Grown as a Fighter, Person," *Los Angeles Times*, November 11, 2001.
19. Mike Krzyzewski, *Leading with the Heart* (New York: Warner Books, 2000), 231.
20. Quoted in David DuPress, "Megastar Still Having a Ball but Future with Bulls Clouded Until After Season," *USA Today*, April 10, 1997.

Chapter 3

1. Ross Newhan, "Tough Act to Follow," *Los Angeles Times*, May 11, 1999: 3.
2. "Sportsmanship in Action," *NFHS News*, November/December 1998.
3. Martin G. Miller, Ph.D., "Developmental Coaching: An Approach to Positive Youth Development in Sports," *New Designs for Youth Development*, Spring 1989, 31.
4. Gough, 12.

5. William Pollack, *Real Boys' Voices* (New York: Random House, 2000), 280–81.
6. John Wooden, *Wooden: A Lifetime of Observations and Reflections on and off the Court* (Chicago: Contemporary, 1997), 94.
7. Jon C. Hellstedt, et al., *On the Sidelines: Decisions, Skills, and Training in Youth Sports* (Amherst, MA: HRD Press, 1988), 85.
8. Bill Plaschke, "Physical Therapy," *Los Angeles Times*, January 23, 1999.
9. Wooden, 53.
10. Sanders, 1–2.
11. Gough, 91–92.
12. Gary Klein, "Worthy of a Salute," *Los Angeles Times*, October 1, 1998.

Chapter 4

1. Chris Sheridan, "Miller Says He Hates Knicks," *Deseret News*, May 23, 2000.
2. Shari Young Kuchenbecker, Ph.D., *Raising Winners: A Parent's Guide to Helping Kids Succeed On and Off the Playing Field* (New York: Times Books, 2000), 61.
3. Clifford and Feezell, 33–34.
4. Stephen Covey, *Principle-Centered Leadership*, 145.
5. Jere Longman, *The Girls of Summer: The U.S. Women's Soccer Team and How It Changed the World* (New York: HarperCollins, 2000), 288.
6. Grant Hill, *Change the Game* (New York: Warner, 1997), 10.
7. Sanders, 141.
8. Bill Plaschke, "Trojans Build a Walk of Shame," *Los Angeles Times*, February 15, 2001.

Chapter 5

1. Quoted in Mary McNamara, "Are We Raging Out of Control?," *Los Angeles Times*, August 6, 2000.
2. Mariah Burton Nelson, *Embracing Victory: Life Lessons in Competition and Compassion* (New York: William Morrow, 1998), 5.
3. Stephen R. Covey, *The 7 Habits of Highly Effective People* (New York: Simon and Schuster, 1989), 207.
4. Nelson, 9.
5. Karan Sims, "Dealing with Power Struggles," positiveparenting.com.
6. Greg Boeck, "Coaching Icon Poised for Another Title Run," *USA Today*, April 21, 2000.
7. Mark Heisler, "NBA Playoffs Passion Play, He Wants to Get Technical About It, So Real Wallace Is Never Seen in Public," *Los Angeles Times*, April 26, 2001.
8. *Olympism: Lighting the Way to a Legacy of Peace*, 67.
9. Amitai Etzioni, " 'Golden Middle' Ends Conflicts," *USA Today*, August 21, 2000.
10. Covey, *The 7 Habits of Highly Effective People*, 9.
11. Robert Lipsyte, "Gesturing by Athletes: The Good, the Bad and the Ugly," *New York Times*, December 12, 1999.
12. Tom Withers, "The Odd Couple," *San Diego Union-Tribune*, May 17, 2000.

Chapter 6

1. Bill Russell, *Russell Rules* (New York: Dutton, Penguin Group, 2001), 141–142
2. Wooden, 93.

3. Mark Burnett with Martin Dugard, *Survivor: The Ultimate Game* (New York: TV Books, 2000), 157.
4. Ed Sherman, "Scotsman Takes the High Road," *Chicago Tribune*, August 20, 1997.
5. Christina Hoff Sommers, "Teaching the Virtues," forerunner.com, September 20, 2000.
6. Quoted in Josie Karp, "Cheating in Baseball Is All Part of Game," *San Diego Union-Tribune*, July 25, 1994.
7. Tim Green, "Cheating to Win Is Rule of Thumb for Teams' Survival," *USA Today*, November 6, 1997.
8. Michael Bamberger and Don Yaeger, "Over the Edge," *Sports Illustrated*, April 14, 1997.
9. Josie Karp, *San Diego Union-Tribune*.
10. Diane Pucin, "Seeking Right or Wrong Answer," *Los Angeles Times*, May 19, 2000.
11. Lumpkin, Stoll, and Beller, 79.
12. Ibid., 68.
13. Wooden, 55.
14. Lumpkin, Stoll, and Beller, 87.
15. Sanders, 176–78
16. Doug Robinson, "Athletes Acting a Lot Like Criminals," *Deseret News*, February 26, 2000.
17. Doug Robinson, "Coach Shocks Folks with Penalty," *Deseret News*, December 6, 1999.
18. Bill Plaschke, "19 Men Out," *Los Angeles Times*, May 25, 2000.
19. Jere Longman, "Two Athletes, an Injury and a Sacrifice," *New York Times*, May 25, 2000.

Chapter 7

1. Quoted in Jill Lieber, "Thompson Wades Right Back In," *USA Today*, August 7, 2000.
2. Sanders, 147.
3. Quoted in Lieber, "Thompson Wades Right Back In."
4. Pantley, 88.
5. Ibid., 89.
6. I talk more in depth about these issues in my book *Beyond the Bleachers: The Art of Parenting Today's Athletes*, written with David Canning Epperson, Ph.D., and published by Alliance Publications, Sugarland, TX.
7. Martin Luther King, Jr., *The Strength to Love* (New York: Harper & Row, 1963), 20.
8. Kuchenbecker, 57–58.

Chapter 8

1. Quoted in Steve Wilstein, "Professional Athletes' Generosity Often Goes Overlooked These Days," *Deseret News*, December 25, 1997.
2. Gary Klein, "Dream Scene," *Los Angeles Times*, November 24, 2001.
3. Steve Brand, "Wiggins Lauded for Act of Generosity," *San Diego Union-Tribune*, April 28, 2001.
4. Adrian Pomery, "Olympic Softball Star Gives Back to Murrieta," *North Crest Times*, July 11, 2000.
5. Stephen R. Covey, *The 7 Habits of Highly Effective Families* (New York: Golden Books, 1997), 185–6.
6. "Sportsmanship in Action," *NFHS News*, March 1999.
7. Kenny Moore, "The Eternal Example," *Sports Illustrated*, December 21, 1992: 16.

8. Samuel Oliner, Pearl M. Oliner, and Harold M. Schulweis, *The Altruistic Personality: Rescuers of Jews in Nazi Europe* (New York: The Free Press, A Division of Macmillan, Inc.) 1992.
9. Debbie Becker, "Skating Queen Kwan Maintains Her Charm," *USA Today*, February 14, 1997.
10. David Wharton, "Golden Boy," *Los Angeles Times*, September 8, 2000.
11. Sanders, 101.
12. Kenny Moore, 16.

Epilogue

1. Quoted in David Goodman, *AP Newsbrief*, October 28, 2000.
2. Al Martinez, "For Whom the Bells Toll," *Los Angeles Times*, July 12, 2000.
3. Tom Pedulla, "Browns Fans Mixed in Reaction," *USA Today*, December 18, 2001.

INDEX